THE HISTORY OF THE
BAKERLOO LINE

THE HISTORY OF THE
BAKERLOO LINE

CLIVE D.W. FEATHER

The Crowood Press

First published in 2020 by
The Crowood Press Ltd
Ramsbury, Marlborough
Wiltshire SN8 2HR

enquiries@crowood.com

www.crowood.com

© Clive D.W. Feather 2020

British Library Cataloguing-in-Publication Data
A catalogue record for this book is available from the British Library.

ISBN 978 1 78500 745 3

FRONTISPIECE: Escalators at St John's Wood; the uplighters are part of the original design.

Typeset by Servis Filmsetting Ltd, Stockport, Cheshire

Printed and bound in India by Parksons Graphics

Contents

Introduction   7

Chapter 1   Before the Bakerloo   10
Chapter 2   Building the Bakerloo   20
Chapter 3   The Wright Stuff   27
Chapter 4   Saved by Yerkes   35
Chapter 5   The Bakerloo Opens   41
Chapter 6   Extending the Line   54
Chapter 7   Improvements   69
Chapter 8   Stanmore   77
Chapter 9   World War II   88
Chapter 10   1950s, 60s and 70s   95
Chapter 11   Jubilee and Beyond   101
Chapter 12   Trains   115
Chapter 13   Signalling   132
Chapter 14   Safety and Danger   140
Chapter 15   Future Plans   147

Line Diagram   149
Appendix I – Dates   150
Appendix II – Proposed names   152
Appendix III – Station Locations and Layouts   152
Index   157

DEDICATION

To my wonderful wife Linda, who has put up with my interests for nearly forty years.

ACKNOWLEDGEMENTS

My thanks to all those who have helped me with data or source material for this book, even if they didn't know why I was asking. I am also grateful to the various people who provided me with photographs and who are named in the captions.

I would particularly like to thank Mark Brader, who has done much fact and consistency checking in my other work over the years, some of which has fed into this book. Charles Dimmock corrected my understanding of the geology of London. Joe Brennan read my first draft and made comments. The Crowood Press first suggested I should write this book and steered me through the process of becoming an author. Finally, my late grandparents took me on the Underground many times as a child and sparked my lifelong interest in it.

A Bakerloo train sits in the reversing siding at Harrow & Wealdstone, the northernmost point of the Bakerloo today.

Introduction

'Bakerloo? Um, that's the brown one, isn't it?'

The Bakerloo is indeed 'the brown one' on London's iconic 'Tube Map'. For the commuter or tourist looking at it, it is simple and boring. It does not have the multiple branches of the Northern or District Lines, the loops of the Piccadilly or the Central, or the puzzling shape of the non-circular Circle. Someone in their fifties might remember that it used to have another branch (someone in their nineties might even remember back to when it didn't). Beyond that, what is there to say about the Bakerloo?

But peek beneath this bland surface and we find much more. This is a line that was conceived by sports enthusiasts, created amongst fraud in the boardroom and drama in the courtroom, finished by Chicago gangsters, and named not by businessmen but by a journalist. An underground railway threatened by weapons in the air in one war between political empires while at the same time being a weapon itself in another war, this time between commercial empires. A place where an enthusiast demonstrated a new way to control trains that, he hoped, would take over the entire country. And, looking ahead, a tool that could renovate a rundown part of London.

My own introduction to the Bakerloo was not as dramatic as this. As a child I would wonder why there were occasional Underground trains in the platforms at Watford Junction when we were waiting for the British Railways (BR) train to London at the start of an outing with my grandparents, or notice that we were using the Bakerloo to reach Stanmore before catching the 142 bus back to Watford at the end of the day. Back then, I was unaware of the rich history behind the Bakerloo Line; it was only as an adult that I became aware of it. But, now that we know it's there, let's wind the clock back more than a century and a half....

'Bakerloo? Um, that's the brown one, isn't it?'

7

A Note on Money and Measurements

Anyone younger than the author probably won't remember that the UK used to use 'pounds, shilling, and pence' as money rather than the newfangled 'decimal currency' brought into use in 1971. Since this book will quote prices in the old money, here's a quick guide to it.

There were twelve (old) pennies in a shilling and twenty shillings in a pound, making a shilling worth 5p and a penny worth just over 0.4p. A sum of four pennies would be written '4d' (note the 'd' rather than 'p'), three shillings would be '3s' or '3/-', and seven shillings and six pennies would be '7s 6d' or '7/6'.

It is not always easy to compare prices from very different times, but, very roughly, the equivalents in 2019 money are:

When	£1	1s	1d
1860–1914	£80 to £90	£4.00 to £4.25	33p to 38p
1920	£30	£1.50	12.5p
1925–39	£45	£2.25	19p
1950	£24	£1.20	10p
1970	£10	50p	4p
1990	£1.60	10p then = 16p now	

Measurements have been given as they appear in the source material, together with the corresponding conversion: for example, rolling stock dimensions are noted in imperial, whereas distances drawn from LU data and OS maps are metric. Historical measurements are generally given in imperial, while more contemporary ones tend to be metric. Conversions are done to an appropriate precision.

Station Names

It is not always clear what is the 'official' name of a station and, indeed, some would claim that there is no such thing. It's certainly not unusual for the same station to have signs with different variations on a name, such as including or excluding apostrophes, or using '&' versus 'and'; in the most extreme case, Piccadilly Circus was just 'Piccadilly' on some signs. In general, this book ignores such variability and sticks with what appears to be the most commonly used version.

Separately from this, several stations have changed names over the years. To avoid confusing the reader too much, present-day names are used throughout, with one exception: because two stations have held the name 'Charing Cross', this book uses 'Trafalgar Square' for the original Bakerloo station at that location (now called 'Charing Cross') and 'Embankment' for the station that originally and currently holds that name, but was called 'Charing Cross' for a while.

Full details of name changes can be found in Appendix I.

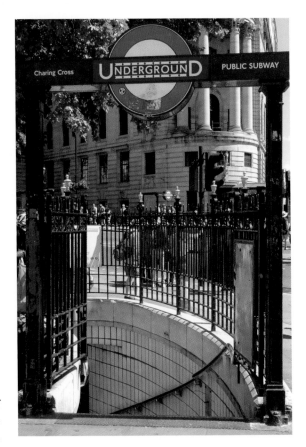

An entrance to Trafalgar Square station, showing its current name of Charing Cross.

Table 1 Abbreviations

Most abbreviations will be obvious from context or are explained when they first occur, but the following table gives the meanings of the more widespread ones.

BR	British Railways (*also called* British Rail)
BS&WR	Baker Street and Waterloo Railway
C&SLR	City and South London Railway
GCR	Great Central Railway (*became part of the LNER in 1923*)
GLC	Greater London Council
GWR	Great Western Railway
IRSE	Institution of Railway Signal Engineers
LER	London Electric Railways
LMSR	London Midland and Scottish Railway
LNER	London and North Eastern Railway
LNWR	London and North Western Railway (*became part of the LMSR in 1923*)
LPTB	London Passenger Transport Board
LSWR	London and South Western Railway
LTE	London Transport Executive
UERL	Underground Electric Railways Company of London

CHAPTER I

Before the Bakerloo

The Bakerloo Line opened in 1906 after a stormy fourteen-year period of planning, construction and crisis that we will see in later chapters. But to understand its origins and the reasons for its construction, we must first look back another forty to fifty years, to London in the middle of the nineteenth century.

In 1860, London had a population of just over 3 million, making it the largest city in the world (second was Beijing, at around 2.6 million); it would double before the end of the century. It had been a port since Roman times and still made much of its money from shipping, though financial services – initially shipping insurance, but then banking and stockbroking – were also important. The centre of London was the City, based around the original Pool of London (the part of the Thames between the modern London and Tower Bridges) and the Bank of England, but it had spread perhaps 5km (3 miles) east and west and 3km (around 2 miles) north and south. In the east, the various dock systems based around the Isle of Dogs had taken over most of the shipping trade, but most of the rest of the growth was residential. Ten or fifteen years earlier the houses of the West End marked London's edge, though by now some tendrils of growth had reached villages like Hammersmith and Putney. To the north, there was continual housing to Kilburn, Camden and Hackney, while to the south Putney,

Clapham and Camberwell marked the edge of the built-up area.

There were three major east–west arteries through western London. The 'New Road' had been built in 1756–7 to allow troops to march around London rather than through it, yet by the turn of the century development was already past it in places. Today we know it variously as Marylebone Road, Euston Road, Pentonville Road, and City Road as it marches from Paddington to Moorgate. The second was Oxford Street and its continuation eastwards as Holborn and Cheapside into the City. This had started life as the Via Trinobantina, a Roman road from Hampshire to Essex, and became a major coaching route as well as the path taken by prisoners from Newgate Prison to execution on the gallows at Tyburn. Finally, the Strand and Fleet Street linked the City to government at Whitehall, Westminster and Buckingham Palace.

By 1860, the railways were firmly settled in London. On the south of the river, London Bridge and Waterloo were well established, Victoria was about to open, and the river crossings to Charing Cross, Blackfriars and Cannon Street were all due to open within the next decade. On the north side, Paddington, Euston, King's Cross and Fenchurch Street were all present, but the Gothic monstrosity of St Pancras would not open until 1868. The lines that now serve Liverpool Street were present,

Tiles on a now-closed entrance to Trafalgar Square present a map of the Oxford Road.

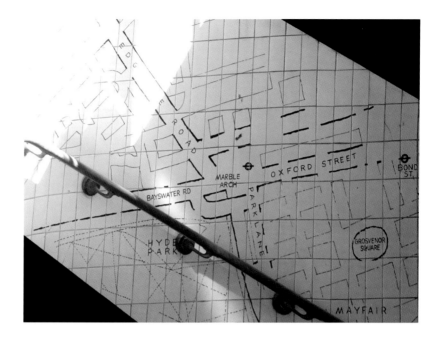

but until 1874 they would terminate 600m (3/8 of a mile) further north at Bishopsgate, on the now-abandoned viaduct just south of the present Shoreditch High Street station. But, though river crossings to both the City and West End were allowed, Parliament had refused since 1846 to allow the railways from the north to cross the New Road.

So how did travellers from Bristol, Birmingham or York get to their destinations in the City or across to catch the boat trains for Dover? How did those from Southampton, Brighton or Canterbury get to offices in Whitehall or houses beside Hyde Park? The answer was the horse-drawn omnibus.

WHY IS IT A 'BUS'?

'Bus' is a contraction of 'omnibus', but where does that come from? Well, the first bus service was introduced by the mathematician Blaise Pascal in 1662, but it was in 1825 that one Stanislaus Baudry started running a bus service in Nantes. Allegedly one terminus was outside the shop of a M Omnès, who had put up a sign '*Omnes omnibus*' – Latin for 'everything for everyone'. More likely, however, is the 1892 claim that Baudry changed the name from 'White Ladies' to 'omnibus cars' ('cars for all') after complaints that the earlier name made no sense.

London had been served by stage coaches for centuries, but the first bus service started in 1829,

running along the New Road to be outside the boundaries of the hackney 'cab' monopoly. Unlike the coaches, the new buses did not have passengers sitting outside on the roof: they were all inside, protected from the weather. But in order to fit in the fourteen passengers that were typical of these services, they were crammed together 'like so many peas in a pod'. Within five years, following changes to the laws and the taxes imposed on them, there were 376 licensed buses in London and passengers were back on the roof again as well as inside.

Today we think of buses as being a cheap form of transport for everyone, but these buses were far from that. Competing with short-distance stage coaches and cabs, the fare was normally 6d for any distance and, as a result, they were far too expensive for the working man. Rather, the typical passenger was the businessman, civil servant or clerk living in Marylebone or Kensington and working near to the Bank or Westminster. It may be interesting to observe that 'manspreading' is not a new phenomenon; on 30 January 1836 *The Times* wrote, 'Sit with your limbs straight, and do not with your legs describe an angle of 45, thereby occupying the room of two persons.'

Typical London horse bus in about 1900.

By the middle of the century, there were around 1,000 buses in competition with each other. Together with perhaps 3,000 cabs and a huge number of vans taking goods between the railway stations on the outskirts and the markets in the middle, the traffic was the kind of continual jam that we think is the fault of the car. Writers complained that it was impossible to cross the road without either being run over or kidnapped by a bus conductor desperate to find fares. One leading businessman stated that he always walked from London Bridge to Trafalgar Square because it was quicker: the cab journey took longer than the train from Brighton had and he could not predict, within a quarter of an hour, how long it would take.

Despite Parliament's ban on railways entering the City, it was obvious that a railway would take much of the strain off the roads and two practical schemes appeared in the early 1850s. The first was the City Terminus Company, headed by Charles Pearson, the City Solicitor. This would involve a road from King's Cross to Holborn with, underneath it, a tunnel containing eight railway tracks. These would connect immediately to the Great Northern at King's Cross, but given that two of the tracks were to be broad gauge it was clear that they were intended to extend to Euston and Paddington. While the Corporation (the government of the City of London) was enthusiastic, the line would be expensive – the route involved buying and then knocking down hundreds or thousands of houses in slums – and nobody was offering the necessary funds.

The second scheme was the North Metropolitan Railway. This solved the cost problem by proposing to dig up the New Road from Paddington to King's Cross, build a tunnel underneath it, then put the road back; no properties to buy reduced the cost dramatically. At King's Cross the line would join the City Terminus line to Holborn. The North

Metropolitan was approved by Parliament in 1853, but the City Terminus was not. After further struggles over the next five years, partly due to opposition in Parliament and elsewhere, and partly because of financial problems, the North Metropolitan took over some of the City Terminus Company's route as far as Farringdon, though on a much smaller scale, and renamed itself the Metropolitan Railway. Between October 1859 and December 1862, various contractors proceeded to build a railway almost completely under the ground and, on Saturday, 10 January 1863, London's – and the world's – first underground line opened for service.

This is not the place for a history of the Metropolitan Railway – though we will meet it again later – or of what is now the Hammersmith & City Line, but its creation showed the world, and in particular those interested in getting around London, three things. First, the ban on railways south of the New Road had been breached and it was possible in principle to build other railways in central London. Second, these railways would be popular and could make money for their creators. But third, and by far the most important, it showed that a new railway did not have to carve an expensive swathe through existing houses, business and shops, but could be built underground with much less disruption using the 'cut and cover' system.

The success of the Metropolitan Railway meant that it was not long before people decided to try other routes. Anyone who studied the bus services would know that north-west London to Westminster and then the Elephant & Castle was popular: even in 1839 there were nine different bus companies with twenty-nine buses between them on the route. And so in 1865 the Waterloo and Whitehall Railway was born.

The Waterloo and Whitehall Railway was planned as a pneumatic railway: a line without locomotives. Instead, trains would be blown through a pipe; to quote the description in *The Times*: 'The tunnel admits a full-sized omnibus carriage, which is impelled by a pressure of the atmosphere behind the vehicle, produced by lessening the density of the air in front.' In other words, an impeller was used to suck out some of the air at one end of the tunnel and normal atmospheric pressure would push the train through the tunnel; on the return journey, the impeller was reversed to generate higher pressure to push the train back.

Pneumatic railways of this kind were not completely new: the idea had been invented by one George Medhurst in around 1810 and a modified version was patented by Thomas Rammell in 1860. Rammell and Josiah Clark established the Pneumatic Dispatch Company, which was to build

Hungerford footbridge – linking Whitehall to Waterloo – in 1859.
JAMES ABBOTT MCNEIL WHISTLER

three lines. A first demonstration tube was built above ground in Battersea in 1861 and used to carry goods and a few hardy volunteers – who would have had to lie down as the tube was only about 75cm (30in) in diameter – at speeds of up to 65km/h (40mph). This gained the interest of the Post Office and the company was engaged to build two lines to carry post and parcels. The first ran from Euston station to the North West District Office, about 500m (1/3 mile) away; the second from Euston to Holborn and thence to the General Post Office (now the BT Centre) near St Paul's Cathedral, a total of about 3.2km (2 miles). The first line operated from 1863 to 1866 and the second from 1865 to 1874 (though only from Euston to Holborn until 1869).

Rammell believed that the system could be used to carry passengers and, on 27 August 1864, he opened a demonstration line in – or rather under – the grounds of the Crystal Palace in Sydenham (now Crystal Palace Park). The line ran from the Sydenham Avenue entrance, probably along the eastern edge of the park, to a point near the eastern end of the Lower Lake. It consisted of a brick 'tunnel' 550m (1,800ft) long; 'tunnel' is in quotes because a 1989 excavation showed that the base of the tube was only 1.5m (5ft) below ground level, so must have sat in a trench with the top half sticking out, possibly disguised with earth. The train

consisted of a single carriage containing thirty-five seats, with a ring of bristles at one end to provide a nearly airtight seal to the tunnel. Despite the sharp curves and the 1 in 15 (6.7 per cent) gradient, far more than a conventional steam train could cope with, the impeller (driven by a modified steam locomotive) only needed to produce a pressure of 2½oz to the square inch (11hPa, or about 1 per cent of atmospheric pressure) to push the train through in about 50 seconds, an average speed of 40km/h (25mph). The demonstration line operated for about two months.

Returning to the Waterloo and Whitehall itself, the idea was to build a pneumatic tube between the two places across the Thames, making the journey much quicker than a bus or cab, which would have to divert via Waterloo Bridge or Westminster Bridge, or a walk over Hungerford Bridge (which cost ½d each way). The proposed route started with an open station at the Whitehall end of Great Scotland Yard, then followed the latter to the river at a point roughly where, today, Whitehall Place meets Whitehall Court (this being before the planned Victoria Embankment had been built). It then crossed the river before running under College Street (now underneath Jubilee Gardens) and Vine Street (destroyed to make way for the 1951 Festival of Britain and now under various buildings) to the

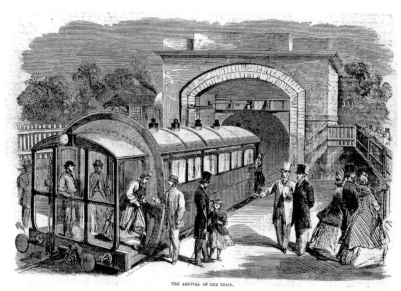

THE ARRIVAL OF THE TRAIN.

Rammell's demonstration pneumatic train arriving at the Sydenham Avenue station. LONDON ILLUSTRATED NEWS COURTESY ROGER J MORGAN

edge of Waterloo Station, at a point that is now part of the erstwhile Eurostar platforms. The total length would have been about 950m (0.6 miles) (most sources quote the length as 1,200m [3/4 mile], but this is not consistent with the route given in the prospectus) and the steepest gradient on the line would be about 1 in 30 (3.3 per cent), significantly less than on the demonstration line. On land, the tunnel would have been cut-and-cover brick construction, while to cross the river it would use an iron tube 12ft 6in (3.81m) in diameter coated in concrete. A trench would be dredged across the river and four brick piers would be sunk into the bed down to the solid clay beneath, each with a chamber at the top. The five tube pieces, sealed at each end, would be lowered into place and inserted into these chambers; it is not clear how they would be fixed together, but possibly by divers. Once all joined up, the seals in the ends could be broken through to give a continuous tunnel. In effect, the result would be a bridge sitting in the riverbed, rather than a pipe sitting on it.

The six initial directors of the company included two directors of the London and South Western Railway (LSWR), which terminated at Waterloo station, and the chairman of the Metropolitan Railway. The former was no doubt attracted by the idea of a good connection to the north side of the river (unlike the other main railways south of the Thames, the LSWR never had a terminus on the north side), while the Metropolitan was probably interested in the technology: despite the usefulness of its line, there were a lot of complaints about the smoke and fug generated by steam engines in the long tunnels. The capital of the company was £135,000 and, as was usual at the time, only a proportion had to be paid up front to buy shares (20 per cent in this case), with the rest being demanded as construction costs required. Some press reports suggested that, if the line was successful, it would become the core of a route from Elephant & Castle to Tottenham Court Road.

The prospectus claimed that a train would run every 4 minutes from each terminus and that trains would alternate in direction. Even if there were two platforms at each end (unlike the demonstration line), so that one train could enter the tunnel as soon as the previous one exited, that would mean a travel time of under 2 minutes, so an average speed of about 31km/h (19mph) with a top speed in the Thames tunnel perhaps 50 per cent greater. Services would run from 07:00 to midnight daily. The company expected trains to carry an average of twenty-five passengers each; 80 per cent would pay 1d for a second-class seat, while the remaining 20 per cent would sit in first class at twice the price. This makes a very exact £23,268 per annum, which would be split 30 per cent for running costs, 12 per cent for interest on the loans taken out to help fund construction, and 58 per cent in dividends, meaning a very comfortable 10 per cent dividend on the shares. The shares would also pay 6 per cent interest – already a very good rate for the time – while the line was being constructed. The prospectus was proud to state that 'its construction will not involve the demolition of a single dwelling-house'; this, of course, meant that no compensation costs would have to be paid to householders or landlords.

The Waterloo and Whitehall's Act of Parliament was passed in 1865 with little or no opposition and construction was started. However, the following May the financial house of Overend, Gurney and Co. collapsed following a drop in stock and bond prices. Overend, Gurney was a major player in the market, certainly bigger than its three biggest competitors combined and with deposits twice those of the Bank of England. The collapse triggered a major financial crisis in London – the 'Panic of 1866' – with the bank rate rising to a then unprecedented 9 per cent and then 10 per cent. The Bank of England had to be reconstituted as the 'lender of last resort' – a role it still holds today – and the panic and resulting recession is credited by some as being the cause of the 1867 Reform Act (which doubled the number of voters by adding many working-class men to the electorate). Meanwhile, the recession meant that it became hard to borrow money – money that the Waterloo and Whitehall needed to fund construction. By 1868, though it had done a fair amount of work, the company had just about given up the

PARLIAMENTARY PROCESS

A railway line can't just be built without anyone's permission unless the entire route is on, or under, land owned by or leased to the company, or land where the owner has given permission (a 'wayleave' – literally 'leave to create a way [through]'). Clearly, it would only take one recalcitrant or greedy landowner to block the line or make it too expensive to build. So up until around the start of the present millennium, railway companies were authorized by a Private Act of Parliament. This Act could grant powers to do things such as to build on or under public lands, to block or reroute roads (either temporarily or permanently), and to open up the route via compulsory purchase, lease or wayleave rights at a fair price, usually determined by an impartial party.

Gaining an Act was far from trivial or cheap. Before the process could start, the promoters needed to put together detailed plans showing exactly where the line would go and what land would be needed for both the line and things like station buildings, goods yards and engine sheds (including a small margin for error). These plans would be accompanied by the Book of Reference, which named the landowner for each piece of land or building affected by the railway. All this paperwork had to conform to Standing Orders issued by Parliament.

Most importantly of all, for a new railway company the promoters needed to determine how much it would cost to build the railway and, therefore, how much money the company would need to raise. This was important because, once the company had its Act, the line could normally only be funded in two ways: either the company sold shares in itself to obtain the money it needed, or it could borrow from banks, other companies or individuals. In general, borrowing was limited to 25 per cent of the total.

Once it was ready, the company had to wait for a narrow window of time, usually in November or December, to deposit the text of its Bill, the plans, the Book of Reference and other necessary documents at the offices of Parliament. Furthermore, the promoters had to deposit 5 per cent of the cost of the new line with approved bankers (this could

be cash or other securities). So, for example, if they decided that the total cost (including an allowance for unforeseen circumstances) would be £200,000, the Bill would set the capital of the new company at £150,000 of shares with borrowing rights of £50,000, while the promoters would have to deposit £10,000 with their paperwork. This deposit would only be returned when the railway was completed and opened, if the Bill failed to get through Parliament, or if a later Act allowed the line to be abandoned.

Once the Bill entered Parliament, it went through the same process as Public Bills (the ones we normally hear about), with each of the two Houses discussing the Bill in turn. A Select Committee of four or five MPs or Lords with no involvement with the line then went through the Bill line by line. They would call witnesses from the promoters, perhaps to justify the line or to explain technical innovations, and from 'petitioners' who objected to the new railway for one reason or another; any of these people might have engaged barristers to help present their position. At the end of this, the committee members discussed things in private before reporting on their conclusions. They announced that the 'preamble' of the Bill (the wording that explains what the Bill is for) was either 'proved' – that is, they agreed with the principle of building the new line – or 'not proved', in which case the proposal was dead for that year. If they found the preamble proved, they might amend the Bill in various ways, either with the agreement of the promoters or over their objections; for example, they could require that a level crossing was replaced by a bridge, or that a tunnel was diverted sideways or downwards to avoid someone's cellars. They usually set a time limit for construction of the line (often leading to further Acts to extend the limit).

In principle, this whole process was gone through twice, once by the Commons and once by the Lords, but in practice whichever House handled it first dealt with the details and the other House only considered the principle.

None of this process was cheap; even at nineteenth-century prices it could cost the company several thousand pounds.

---

effort. A further blow was struck by the opening in January 1869 of what is now Waterloo East station, creating a rail service between Waterloo and Charing Cross. The line was officially abandoned in 1870 and the surplus machinery and materials were auctioned off in 1872. The company was eventually wound up in 1882. It is claimed (though there is no solid evidence) that part of the W&W's tunnels is now in use by the National Liberal Club as its wine cellar. With this possible exception, all evidence of the line has gone, though part of the tunnels under Vine Street were discovered in the early 1960s when excavating foundations for the Shell Centre.

THE END OF PNEUMATIC RAILWAYS?

The W&W was the only pneumatic passenger railway to be built, or rather part-built, in the UK, but Rammell was involved in various further proposals for pneumatic railways under London, none of which gained their Act of Parliament. In the USA, however, the concept was taken up by Alfred Ely Beach, the publisher of Scientific American. He first built a demonstration line in 1867 and then in 1870 opened a public line under New York's Broadway some 312ft (95m) long, making it New York's first underground railway. Though Beach planned a line 8km (5 miles) long, official and political opposition meant that it was never extended beyond the first section and closed in 1873. The tunnels have gone and the route of the line is now almost entirely within the New York Subway's City Hall station. However, it made a spectacular, if unrealistic, reappearance in the 1989 film Ghostbusters II.

A piece of the Waterloo and Whitehall's under-river tunnel during construction. SCIENTIFIC AMERICAN COURTESY JOSEPH BRENNAN

In 1881, there was a second attempt to build a railway from Waterloo to the north side of the Thames near Whitehall: the Charing Cross and Waterloo Electric Railway, launched by (among others) two directors of the Great Eastern Railway.

The Charing Cross and Waterloo was aiming at the same market as the Waterloo and Whitehall: people wanting to get across the Thames from Waterloo station to the general area of Trafalgar Square. For this reason, its design and route were very similar. It started at an open station at the edge of Waterloo station. The lines then descended into a cut-and-cover tunnel under Vine Street and then College Street to reach the Thames, descending at a 3 per cent (1 in 33) gradient all the way. On the north bank of the Thames it would then climb at 2.4 per cent (1 in 42) under Northumberland Avenue; this had been driven from Embankment to Trafalgar Square in 1874, replacing the former Northumberland House and its grounds. The terminus would be 20ft (6m) below ground level just before the junction with the square itself, opposite the Grand Hotel under construction at the time. The line would cross the Thames in two iron tubes in trenches, as with the W&W. However, the use

of Northumberland Avenue meant that the river crossing would take a noticeable diagonal. The total length would be about 1km (⅝ mile).

The big difference from the Waterloo and Whitehall, however, was the form of traction. Pneumatic tubes were a dead duck, but it was no longer necessary to revert to steam. Dr Werner von Siemens had shown that it was practical to haul at least a small train using an electric locomotive powered from a fixed generator. In 1879, he built a demonstration line consisting of a loop 300m (330 yards) in length with a small locomotive pulling three carriages holding eighteen to twenty people each at about 12km/h (7½mph). It used a central third rail or, rather, a vertical iron plate, with the return through the running rails. In 1881, this was moved to Crystal Palace Park; at the same time, Siemens was building a 2.5km (1.6 miles) passenger line on the outskirts of Berlin and was proposing a 10km (6 miles) elevated line within the city, both electrified (but using the two running rails to carry power, like a model railway). Dr Siemens also pointed out that the electric motor in the locomotive could brake the train by becoming a generator, a technique still in common use today. In two years' time, the first electric railway in the UK –

Volk's Electric Railway on the Brighton shoreline; the first electric railway in the UK.

Volk's Electric Railway – would open in Brighton; it is still running today.

The promoters of the Charing Cross and Waterloo leapt on the idea of electric trains and gained Siemens Brothers as backers, with Dr Carl Wilhelm Siemens (a younger brother of Werner) as electrical engineer. Their prospectus pointed out the advantages of electric traction, with clean air and no smoke in the tunnels. The trains would be single lightweight self-propelled carriages with no locomotives.

The company's initial Act of Parliament obtained Royal Assent on 18 August 1882, but the attempts to sell shares and so raise money only started in the following April. The capital of the company was £100,000; again, only 20 per cent had to be paid up front to buy shares and the rest would be demanded as construction costs required. This time it was made explicit that each demand would be no more than 20 per cent of the share price and would be made at least three months apart, allowing prospective buyers to plan their cash flow. The company could also borrow up to £33,000. Contractors had been found who would build the line for £80,000 and Siemens Brothers wanted £12,000 for the electrical equipment (the generator to supply power would be beside the Waterloo station).

The prospectus again described the expected service. The running time was 3½ minutes, making the average speed only about half that of the Waterloo and Whitehall, and there was no timetable: trains would 'start as filled' (presumably empty or part-empty trains would be sent back if there was more demand in one direction than the other, just as in rush-hour today). The company expected to carry 12,000 passengers per day, with one-third in first class paying 2d and the rest in second class paying 1d; these were the same prices as the W&W, but with more in the expensive seats. The company's Act actually allowed for three classes at fares up to 6d, 4d and 3d but, presumably, it was decided that these higher rates would discourage too many potential passengers. If these targets could be met, the company would earn £24,333 per annum; Siemens Brothers would be paid £5,867 to provide and run the trains (they had a five-year contract that paid them £5,000 plus 20 per cent of any income over £20,000 each year), which, after deducting £4,000 in maintenance and management expenses, would mean a very impressive 14.5 per cent dividend for the shareholders. On the other hand, unlike the W&W, there was no offer of interest while the line was being built. In an attempt to justify these figures, the prospectus pointed out that there were 22,106 carriages and 93,274 pedestrians crossing the three bridges in the area each day, but failed to remind investors that the crossing was now free: the Metropolitan Board of Works had purchased Waterloo Bridge and the toll rights of Hungerford Bridge in 1878, abolishing the tolls.

Even before any significant work had started, the company was looking at extensions. A December 1882 Bill proposed extending from Waterloo via Blackfriars to the Royal Exchange, roughly following the route of today's Waterloo & City Line and trebling the length of the line. An extra £336,000

Hungerford Railway Bridge in 1890. CAMILLE PISSARRO

would be required for this. This idea was dropped in May 1883. Instead, Siemens Brothers were promoting the London Central Electric Railway, which would have extended the Charing Cross and Waterloo from Trafalgar Square north to meet Oxford Street near Holborn and then eastwards along the route of the present Central Line to the Post Office (present-day St Paul's). Parliament rejected this as too speculative, wanting to see if the CC&WER worked first. But the latter was in trouble. Attempts to sell its shares had not gone well and it could not afford to undertake any construction (apparently only about 20m [66ft] of tunnel was ever built). Then, in December 1883, Dr Siemens died, removing one of the driving forces of the line. In November 1884, the company brought two separate Bills to Parliament. One would allow the line to be extended along Cockspur Street to '85 yards west of the statue of Charles I' (in other words, to the south-west corner of Trafalgar Square) and would

extend the time allowed for construction. The other, however, would allow the entire railway to be abandoned. It was this latter that received Royal Assent on 16 July 1885, sounding the death knell for the line.

One more railway proposal should be mentioned: the King's Cross, Charing Cross and Waterloo Subway, which would have been much more like a modern tube line than the previous ones. This 1885 proposal followed the route of the CC&WER from Waterloo to Northumberland Avenue, though the station would be at the junction with Northumberland Street. From there, it would run along the east side of Trafalgar Square, then under St Martin's Street, Long Acre, Great Queen Street, Southampton Row, Theobolds Road and Gray's Inn Road to King's Cross, a total of 2 miles 13.8 chains (3.5km). The promoters withdrew the proposal in May of the same year and it was not raised again.

CHAPTER 2

Building the Bakerloo

Iron and Clay

The tube lines under London were made possible by one invention and one piece of fortuitous geology. The invention was the tunnelling shield. The first version was patented in 1818 jointly by Marc Brunel (builder of the first tunnel under the Thames and father of Isambard Kingdom Brunel) and Admiral Lord Cochrane (a colourful character nicknamed 'the Sea Wolf' by Napoleon and who was the partial inspiration for the fictional character Horatio Hornblower). It is usually claimed that Brunel was inspired by the tunnelling ship-worm *Teredo navalis*. The shield Brunel actually used was rectangular and it fell to three people to improve it. Alfred Beach, who we met in the previous chapter, suggested in 1840 that a cylinder was better and used one to build his pneumatic railway, though this does not appear to have become well known until 1870. There were then two further patents: independently of Brunel, Peter Barlow FRS (engineer for various railways including the South Eastern and designer of the first Lambeth Bridge) patented a cylindrical shield in 1864, but never used it in practice. This was left to his South African pupil James Greathead, whose design (patented in 1874) was used to construct the second tunnel under the Thames – the 1869 Tower Subway from Tower Hill to Vine Lane – and the seven 'tube' railways that

would serve London for the next century, including the Bakerloo.

The tunnelling shield itself is a very simple invention. It consists of a thin-walled metal cylinder at the front end of the tunnel under construction. If the tunnel is being dug by hand, as it was in Greathead's time, miners would excavate material from inside the shield to create the tunnel. When the excavated space is large enough, the shield is moved forward by screw jacks or hydraulic rams (Alfred Beach was the first person to use the latter), pushing against the lining of the completed tunnel. This reveals enough space inside the shield to build a further section of the lining. Since the weight of the ground above (the 'overburden') will be trying to collapse the tunnel, there is no time to build a brick lining, which would take several days to set, meaning that the shield could only be moved one ring every few weeks. Instead, a faster technique must be used: traditionally, a number of iron segments were fitted together to form a ring of the tunnel wall, though pre-cast concrete segments would work equally well. In either case, a typical ring might be 50cm (20in) long. All this time, of course, the shield is holding back the overburden and protecting the tunnellers installing the new ring. As soon as the ring is in place, it will be possible to move the shield again. Even working by hand, a seasoned crew can install a new

James Greathead's statue outside Bank station.

a more recent technique involves expanding the segments outwards to push them into the surrounding material, meaning that grouting is either unnecessary or involves much less work (this has to be done behind the shield rather than within it, and so is only suitable for tunnels in hard material that will not collapse before the ring can be assembled). A good tunnelling team can easily average 6in (15cm) an hour.

DUNN'S PATENT

There was another early patent for a cylindrical tunnelling shield, issued to Samuel Dunn of Doncaster in 1849. Unlike both Brunel's and Greathead's shields, the front of the shield was not a workface for miners, but, rather, was wedge-shaped, rather like the front of a streamlined train. As with other shield designs, a pneumatic ram pushing on the completed tunnel forced the wedge into the ground being tunnelled, with new sections of tunnel lining being assembled in the rear part of the shield. Because material was pushed away from the shield rather than being excavated, it would only have been useful in soft sand or mud and there is no record of the design being used. However, it was the first ever description of a shield that moved forward in one piece like Barlow's, rather than many separate pieces like Brunel's.

This leads to 'the accident of geology'. There is an irregular area in southern England roughly bounded by Hungerford, Dartford, Harwich and Ipswich; just about all of Greater London and Essex lie within it and the Thames from Reading eastwards flows across it. This area is the home of the London Clay, also known as the Blue Clay.

The rocks under London mostly formed in the Cretaceous period – the second half of the time of the dinosaurs – between about 145 and 66 million years ago. The most important part of these rocks is a layer, up to 200m (660ft) thick, of chalk; this is the same chalk that forms the white cliffs of Dover. This chalk lies on top of impervious rocks and so carries large amounts of water, with wells sunk into this layer providing much of London's water. Just after the extinction of the dinosaurs, an event called the Alpine orogeny started. The major effect of this was to push up land to form the Alps but, as a side effect, it caused vertical movements in southern England.

ring and fix it to the existing tunnel in half an hour or so. Once the shield has moved forward another time or two, it will no longer be enclosing the ring. At this point, it is necessary to fill the space that the shield had occupied, or else the buildings or road above will eventually subside into it. This traditionally involves injecting grout into the space through small holes left in the rings for the purpose, though

At the time, this area was under a shallow subtropical sea fringed by lush forests; sand and silt in the sea formed a layer of clays and sands about 8–24m (25–80ft) thick, often containing oyster shells, on top of the chalk. These layers are known to geologists as the Lambeth Group, though the mixture of colours and embedded mottled pebbles caused early tunnellers to call it the 'Shepherd's Plaid'. However, the movements of the Alpine orogeny caused London to sink and the Chilterns and North Downs to rise. This allowed the London area to fill with Ypresian (early Eocene) clay in the period between 56 and 48 million years ago. This is the London Clay and it in turn sits on the Lambeth Group.

London Clay is a silty clay with some sandy and pebble beds in it. The layer under London is up to 130m (430ft) thick with its top typically between 10 and 50m (30–160ft) below ground level, though there are places where it is shallower and it actually comes to the surface in a few areas. It contains a relatively large amount of ferrous oxide, giving it a blue-grey colour and its name of Blue Clay. Once exposed, the ferrous oxide will react with oxygen in the air to form ferric oxide, changing the colour of the clay to brown. The London Clay includes a large range of fossils, including palm fruits, molluscs and crocodiles. However, for our purposes its most important property is that it is stiff, but relatively soft. What this means is that it's relatively easy to tunnel through even by hand, unlike granite or other hard rocks, but, on the other hand, the tunnel won't immediately try to collapse around the hood before the next ring of lining can be assembled. This makes it an ideal material to dig through and most of the tunnels under London – not just the Underground tube lines – go through the clay.

Having looked at shields, iron tubes and clay, we can now return from the time of the dinosaurs and other prehistoric beasts to the nineteenth century.

Planning the Bakerloo

By 1890, the Metropolitan Railway had grown and been joined by its sister company, the Metropolitan District Railway (now the District Line). Between them, with a lot of struggles that are outwith the scope of this book, the two companies had managed to create the Inner Circle around the central area of London, together with branches into the suburbs. However, they had also made it clear that cut-and-cover was not practical any more: the last part of the Circle (the 1.82km [6,000ft] from Mansion House to Aldgate) cost each company £1.25 million, plus grants of nearly another million pounds.

This piece of tunnelling shield used at Bank station in 1898 was exposed during work in 1987 and now forms part of a pedestrian tunnel.

St John's Wood, closest station to Lord's Cricket Ground, with a mismatched addition on top.

Though the Inner Circle had eased road congestion for a while, it was not a long-term panacea. In the decade from 1881 to 1891, the population of Greater London grew by 20 per cent. This increase meant that the traffic in central London had reached chaotic proportions, with a 28 per cent growth in the number of vehicles entering London and an eye-watering 68 per cent growth in horse buses. By 1900, there would be 690 buses an hour at Bank and 622 at Piccadilly Circus; even Kilburn was seeing 83 buses an hour. The time was ripe for something better.

There had been many proposals for lines through the central area – usually underground – several of which got as far as approval by Parliament, but at this point only one had actually been built and opened. This was the City and South London Railway (C&SLR) from Stockwell to King

William Street (close to the Monument), opened on 18 December 1890. This was seen by many as an experimental line because of the number of innovations it introduced, and it was far from successful financially (it paid no dividends in its first year and by 1897 had only reached 2 per cent), but it was the first electrically powered tube line in London and the world. Even now, most of its original length is part of the Northern Line. It was the pioneer that led to the Bakerloo and the other tube lines criss-crossing central London today.

At the end of 1891, the published list of Parliamentary Bills for the 1892 session included (as well as one for the Channel Tunnel) the Baker Street and Waterloo Railway (BS&WR). This proposal, it was later claimed, was dreamt up by a group of businessmen who worked in the Westminster area and were cricket fans. They were upset that it

THE OTHER 1892 PROPOSALS

The other new lines consisted of: the Great Northern and City Railway (now the East Coast Main Line branch from Finsbury Park to Moorgate); the Hampstead, St Pancras and Charing Cross Railway (now, with some changes, the section of the Northern Line from Hampstead to Charing Cross); and the Waterloo & City Railway (now the Waterloo & City Line). The two extensions now form the section of the Central Line from Bank to Liverpool Street and the section of the Northern Line between Angel and Borough.

was not practical to get to Lord's after work to see the end of the day's play because of the slow speed of buses or cabs in the heavy traffic. In looking into the possibility of faster travel, they realized that there was a large demand for travel along a north–south axis and an underground railway line could, therefore, be made profitable. This is certainly a very pretty story and might well be true, though it does not seem to have appeared until 1906.

As might be deduced from its name, the BS&WR would run from the existing Baker Street station roughly south to Waterloo station; the detailed route will be described later. The 1892 session of Parliament was faced with proposals for four new underground lines and extensions to two others. Furthermore, since the C&SLR had been running for just over fourteen months when Parliament started to consider the Bills, there was an opportunity to learn lessons from this first tube line and ensure that any mistakes it had made were avoided. Therefore it was decided to abandon the usual approach of discussing each Bill separately and, instead, a Joint Committee of the Commons and Lords was set up to consider all four together.

The Joint Committee reached a number of conclusions. All four new lines would relieve the problems with surface traffic and would facilitate the expansion of London outwards. They would not obstruct any proposed or likely future railways and so all four Bills could be processed by Parliament in the ordinary way. The Joint Committee also set down a number of general rules and principles for both these and other future railways under

London, the most important of which was that the companies should be entitled to wayleaves (permission to build) under both streets and properties, the former for free, provided that landowners were properly compensated for any damage caused by the construction or operation of the line; the *quid pro quo* for this was that the companies had to run 'an adequate number of cheap and convenient trains'.

On technical matters, the Joint Committee confirmed that all such railways should be built to standard gauge (4ft 8½in or 1,435mm). Electric trains were the right approach to take, though places with steep gradients might benefit from cable traction (where the train grips on to a continuously moving cable driven by a fixed engine). Tunnels were to be at least 11ft 6in (3.54m) in internal diameter, rather larger than the C&SLR, though they rejected the proposal of the London County Council for a diameter of 16ft (4.88m) to allow main-line trains to run through them.

In respect of the BS&WR in particular, most of the opposition was relatively minor and involved specific concerns. A number of landowners along Northumberland Avenue – from the Grand Hotel at one end to the National Liberal Club at the other – were concerned about 'the exceptional character of the buildings and soil'. It was agreed that, as well as the usual rules for compensating property owners for any damage done, the tops of any tunnels (including station tunnels) would be at least 10ft (3m) below the upper surface of the London Clay throughout the length of Northumberland Avenue, no electricity generating stations were to be built within 100yd (90m) of any of the petitioners' properties, and the petitioners could appoint an engineer empowered to inspect the work in progress and require the company to take appropriate precautions. The Thames Conservators wanted to make a profit from the rights to allow the railway to run under the river, but were refused. The Crown Estate and the Portland Estate clearly did not want easy access to their lands, resulting in a ban on any station between Baker Street and Oxford Circus.

There eventually was a station between Baker Street and Oxford Circus, but access required walking along one of these rather dramatic tunnels.

However, there were two major objectors: the Metropolitan Railway and the South Eastern Railway (SER). These two companies had the same chairman, Sir Edward Watkin, who also ran the Manchester, Sheffield and Lincolnshire Railway. This latter had a Bill going through Parliament to build an extension from Sheffield to London, which was intended to connect to the Metropolitan and thence the SER. The main concern of the Metropolitan was that this connection was intended to be a second pair of tracks beneath the Inner Circle, rather than digging up Euston Road again to widen the existing cut-and-cover tunnel, and they did not want to be blocked by 'a little electric omnibus line'. The SER, on the other hand, were hoping to extend their line from Charing Cross northwards to the Euston / St Pancras / King's Cross area to create a north–south route across London; the BS&WR would therefore be both an obstruction and a competitor. The joint counsel for the two lines was vehement in his language: the BS&WR 'would be absolutely and totally useless for ordinary railway traffic,

and a useless and stupid line which would have next to no traffic, even if it were ever made' and was 'an omnibus service which could not possibly be made to pay'. Despite this rhetoric, plus delays caused by a General Election, Parliament approved the Bill and it gained Royal Assent on 28 March 1893.

Raising the Finance

Having an Act of Parliament was only the first stage in the story. Next, the company needed to raise money. However, this was much easier said than done. The authorized share capital was £1,250,000 (with borrowing powers of £416,000). On its own, it might have been possible to find this money, but the BS&WR was one of six tube lines in London all looking for money at the same time. As a result, the company found itself without enough money to carry out any serious work – its estimates had been that constructing the line would cost £900,000, while trains, lifts and other equipment would cost another £330,000.

In an attempt to court the GCR, Marylebone station was even originally named after it.

In 1896, the company went back to Parliament to ask for an extension of time, but also to extend the line at its western end from Baker Street to the south-east corner of Harewood Square, which was about to disappear underneath the new Marylebone station being built for the Great Central Railway (GCR). This would give the GCR a connection to the network of underground lines under construction, particularly those south of the Thames, rather than requiring its passengers to walk to Baker Street. This Act was passed with little difficulty, but it did not encourage investors to come forward. Even though the BS&WR shared two directors with the LSWR, the latter clearly did not think there would be enough traffic to make it worthwhile. (This was probably a shrewd decision on their part, since passengers from Sheffield and Manchester to the south-west would probably travel via Birmingham rather than London.)

Late in November 1897, a Bill was introduced to Parliament by James Heath, a Conservative MP. This was for the New Cross and Waterloo Railway. However, despite its name suggesting that it was a completely separate line, it was actually a proposal to more than double the length of BS&WR at its south end. The new route would diverge from the existing one just south of the Thames and run along

Waterloo Road, in front of Waterloo station, down to the Elephant & Castle, then along the New and Old Kent Roads to the London, Brighton and South Coast Railway's station (this is now closed, but lay roughly midway between Queen's Road Peckham and South Bermondsey stations, just south of where the East London Line joins the line from London Bridge). The original BS&WR route under Waterloo station would be retained to provide access to the depot, which would be roughly where the present Waterloo & City Line depot is situated, and would be extended to rejoin the new line near Gray Street. This would involve nine new stations compared with the seven on the original route.

More interesting, however, was the second part of the proposal, which would involve a junction immediately north of the Euston Road and a new branch under Longford Street and Drummond Street to the east side of Euston station, with an intermediate stop north of the present Warren Street station.

The company would have been capitalized at £975,000, with £325,000 of borrowing powers. Fares would have been 2d per mile in first class and 1d per mile in second. Its main market would have been the passengers on the horse trams along the same route. However, despite some enthusiasm from the specialist press, the Bill made no progress in Parliament and disappeared.

CHAPTER 3

The Wright Stuff

November 1897 was a key month for the BS&WR. On the fourth of that month, the directors signed an agreement with the London and Globe Finance Corporation (L&G), a creation of Whitaker Wright. Under this deal, the L&G agreed to build and equip the entire line for the sum of £1,766,000 (three-quarters in BS&WR shares and the rest in the company's debenture stock). The L&G then immediately turned round and agreed to pay Perry & Co. of Bow £877,000, or slightly under half this amount, to actually build the line. Given that this was just about all of the company's capital, within a few weeks the BS&WR's board of directors had been replaced by one identical to the L&G's.

Now that someone with actual money was involved with the BS&WR, construction could finally begin. The work started in August 1898 by building a large wooden pier in the Thames just west of Hungerford Bridge, with several buildings and lots of machinery on it, including a small generating station to power equipment and also allow the tunnels to be lit during the work. From here, two vertical shafts were sunk down into the London Clay to allow tunnelling to start. The use of this pier avoided the need for (and cost of) obtaining land in central London to work from and also meant that spoil from the tunnel could be shipped out by barge rather than on wagons that would block roads. Digging towards Baker Street started the following February, with the

WHITAKER WRIGHT

James Whitaker Wright was born in 1846 in Stafford, the son of a Methodist minister. At fifteen, he had a job as a printer and at eighteen he became a Methodist minister himself, though he retired after a couple of years, claiming ill health.

By the late 1860s he had moved to the USA. Starting as a gold and silver prospector, he realized that the real money was to be made in finance, not in digging. He started buying up silver mines, promoting them heavily and selling them for a large profit (though the buyers were to find that the mines were loss-making; as Wright once told a friend: 'The people want to be skinned, and I am going to skin them.'). By the age of thirty-one, he was a millionaire, though he was to lose his fortune when one of his companies went bust.

Wright fled to London in 1889 to avoid his creditors and, possibly, criminal charges. There he started again, dealing in mining shares. The discovery of gold in Western Australia in 1892 put him in a commanding position: he was one of the first to buy up large numbers of mining leases that could be developed into (so people hoped) profitable mines. By the late 1890s, Wright was the richest man in England and, possibly, the entire world. He bought the 9,000-acre (3,600 hectares) Witley Park in Surrey (then called Lea Park) and turned it into a lavish mansion and grounds, with three separate artificial lakes, a revolving glass dome and even an underwater conservatory, still in existence today.

In 1894 and 1895 Wright formed 'holding' companies to invest in the shares of mining companies; shares of these holding companies were popular and, at least for Wright, profitable. In 1897, he merged these companies into a single organization, the London and Globe Finance Corporation, with a capital of 2 million pounds. Wright was an expert in recruiting famous names as directors to build public confidence in his companies: the chairman of the L&G was Frederick Hamilton-Temple-Blackwood, 1st Marquess of Dufferin and Ava, formerly Governor General of Canada and Viceroy of India.

Wright's younger brother John also has a transport connection: while living in Toronto he invented the reversible trolley pole still used on many tram and trolleybus systems.

The banks of the Thames at Hungerford Bridge, showing the approximate path of the Bakerloo tunnels.

tunnels towards Waterloo starting some thirteen months later.

In November of 1898, a year after the L&G take-over, the BS&WR presented a new Bill to Parliament for consideration in the 1899 session. This would involve an extension and a branch, plus a minor adjustment to the route at the Waterloo end to reach a new depot site. The extension was to Paddington, with a station under Paddington Basin and a depot on the surface in Little Venice. The branch was to Euston, but not on the same route as the previous year's proposal. Instead it was further north, running under Cumberland Market at Varndell Street to terminate at the north-west corner of

Euston station. This branch would have meant that the three-minute service on the line would be split equally between the two northern termini, with a six-minute service to each. The cost of the new works would have been £1,090,000 and other expenses £525,000.

The Metropolitan Railway promptly had conniptions, viewing this as direct competition to the Inner Circle and objecting strenuously in Parliament. The Select Committee were also concerned by the large amount of extra capital to be issued, worried that this was simply a plan by the L&G to make a quick profit. The promoters responded that, although the authorized capital was £1,766,000, the costs of £1,615,000 meant that they would receive less than 10 per cent profit, which was not unreasonable. However, this time the Metropolitan got its way and both extension and branch were rejected; the final Act only allowed the adjustment at Waterloo, subways at Trafalgar Square to various street corners, and an extension of time.

Despite this failure in Parliament, construction continued throughout 1899. At the L&G's AGM it was stated that £384,441 had been spent so far on the works (shareholders need not be concerned, as the line could easily be sold to another railway at any time). With work in progress and an income in distant sight, the company decided to have another go at the northern extensions. This time, the Paddington station would be under Bishop's Bridge Road, with a long subway under Eastbourne Terrace (a site now occupied by the Elizabeth Line station) to the Great Western Railway (GWR) station, while the Euston branch would start at Oxford Circus this time. Finally, the southern end of the line would be extended to Elephant & Castle – though not along the same route as the New Cross and Waterloo had proposed – with a subway connection to the C&SLR station there. There would be no intermediate stations on the Elephant extension, but one on the west side of Edgware Road on the way to Paddington. The BS&WR had also reached agreement with the trustees of the School for the Indigent Blind, who had been looking for an opportunity to move to the countryside; the site would

be used for a generating station and a depot, with a branch tunnel to the main route. An extra million pounds worth of shares would be issued and the borrowing limit extended by £333,000. The L&G would get 97 per cent of the capital raised from selling the shares, but it would carry all the risk of the extension work and would make only £100,000 profit. The depot site would cost £299,000.

The GWR, GCR and LSWR all approved of the Paddington extension and supported it in Parliament (the Euston branch seems to have been dropped at an early stage). The general manager of the LSWR said that 'it was a blot upon London that there was such a lack of communication between the great railway termini'. The general manager of the GWR went into detail: at present it cost 2/6 and three-quarters of an hour to take a cab between Paddington and Waterloo, while the railway would do it in sixteen minutes for 2d; even a bus would cost 5d for a much slower journey. (He did reserve the right, though, to propose a more direct line to Charing Cross in the future.) The Metropolitan attacked the Paddington proposal once again. This time, their approach was to describe the experiments with electrification that they were carrying out together with the Metropolitan District that, they said, showed that there was no need for another line between Paddington and Baker Street (this section was not actually electrified until July 1905). They also attacked the financial arrangements with the L&G. But this time Parliament was not convinced and the Act received Royal Assent on 6 August.

Prospectus

With this new Act under its belt and the support of the L&G in its pocket, the BS&WR finally issued a Prospectus on 10 November 1900. There were 238,500 shares for sale at £10 each; 6,600 of these were 4 per cent preference shares and the rest ordinary shares (this meant that, if there was just a small profit, only the preference shareholders would get a dividend, while the ordinary shareholders would get nothing, but if the profits were

The Metropolitan eventually had to live with the Bakerloo; signs on their platforms at Baker Street.

big enough, the preference shares would receive 4 per cent per annum of the share value, while the ordinary shareholders would share out the rest, whether that be more or less than 4 per cent). Once again, investors were not required to put up all the money up front (though there was a specific note that they could do so), just £4 per share, with the other £6 being demanded as the company needed the money – calls would be for not more than £2 per share each time and would be at least three months apart. (It was also noted that failure to pay these calls could result in the shareholder losing the shares without compensation.) During construction, the company would pay shareholders 3 per cent per annum on the money they had actually paid out so far. The company had existing or planned loans via debentures of £794,000 at 4 per cent per annum.

There was a detailed description of progress so far. Starting at the river stage (the temporary pier), the northbound tunnel (still referred to using the conventional railway terminology as the 'down' line) had reached the junction of Regent Street and Air Street, while the southbound had reached the north end of Northumberland Avenue plus a short section through Piccadilly Circus. In the other direction, the northbound was almost across the river after delays caused by water-bearing gravel. Separate work at Baker Street had dug the north-

bound from the west side of Baker Street station to the start of the turn to cross the Euston Road and the southbound under Baker Street station itself. Lift shafts had been sunk at Baker Street and Piccadilly Circus and were in progress at Waterloo. Five station tunnels were complete – southbound at Baker Street and Embankment, both at Piccadilly Circus, and one at Trafalgar Square with the other part-done. The average speed would be 13mph (21km/h) including stops, meaning that the journey between Paddington and Elephant & Castle would take 25 minutes instead of the 75 that a bus would take.

Statistics were thrown around to encourage investors. The five biggest points of concentration of passenger traffic in London were Bank, Elephant & Castle, Charing Cross, Piccadilly Circus and then Oxford Circus, and the line would serve four of them. Passing along shopping districts, government offices, hotels, theatres, business centres and 'one of the most densely populated Artisan Districts in London' meant that the line was not reliant on peak traffic, but would have business throughout day and night. Waterloo saw 28 million passengers a year, while Baker Street saw 15 million coming from the Metropolitan's main line (that is, ignoring passengers on the Inner Circle), so there should be a large number travelling between the two. Running costs would be £100,000 a year, assuming 300 trains each way on weekdays and half that on Sunday (in those times Saturday was a normal working day). The passenger income was estimated at £260,000 and other income at £10,000. Subtracting costs and interest on the loans would leave £138,240 in dividends, meaning more than 6 per cent dividends on the ordinary stock. There was room for growth: the stations were 50 per cent longer than needed for the initial trains. To date, the L&G had spent exactly £654,705 10s 7d on building the line.

Collapse of London and Globe

But very soon things started to go wrong. At the end of November, shares of L&G were at 20s 6d (that is, 2.5 per cent above their face value), but went into decline: they were 18s 6d on 10 December and 17s on the evening of Friday the fourteenth. The following Monday was the Annual General Meeting of the company. At a very crowded meeting, the shareholders heard that difficulties in the markets would mean that no dividends would be paid this year. This was, the chairman said, partly due to the Boer War depressing the stock market in general, but also partly due to their involvement in the BS&WR. Unlike their normal business, this required paying out real money and the company's resources needed to be husbanded. When shareholders asked why they had gone into this business, the blame was carefully pushed on to two former directors, both now deceased, while still suggesting that it was a good investment. By the following evening, the shares were down to 14s, though they recovered the next day to 15s 6d, but by 28 December they were down to 13s.

On Saturday 29 December, there were reports of the collapse of the share price of several Western Australian mining companies, all of which the L&G was involved with, and some thirteen share traders went into default (this is, were unable to pay money they owed). On the Monday – the last day of the century – the L&G issued a notice convening a meeting to consider going into voluntary liquidation. The reason given was that the company's capital was tied up in securities that could not be converted into cash, making it impossible to carry on business. The share price responded to this move by dropping again, to 6s 6d, or just under one-third of face value. *The Times* suggested that some of the L&G's assets were better described as liabilities and reported that the Stock Exchange Committee was taking measures to override this 'rather impudent proposal'; a winding-up petition was issued the next day.

A rumour went round on 4 January that the BS&WR had been sold to somebody for £400,000 (that is, less than two-thirds of what had been spent on it so far), with the LSWR and a Mr Yerkes both being named, though *The Times* reported that it could confirm that neither of them had done so and by the next day the rumour seems to have died. On 14 January an Extraordinary General Meeting of the L&G agreed to put the company into voluntary liquidation with creditors getting about 50 per cent of what they were owed. Within a few days, the shares had hit a new low of 3s 3d. The winding-up order was rejected by the court, but a subsequent one was granted on 30 October.

As the liquidation process carried on, some curious facts started to come out of the woodwork. There had been complaints that the EGM was called so quickly that creditors did not have time to find shareholders that might support them. These creditors wanted a neutral liquidator rather than one picked by Wright, fearing that the story behind the troubles would not be investigated. At the EGM, Marquess Dufferin resigned as Chairman, after having explained that he did not understand the business of the company and relied on Wright to run it. Evidence emerged that Wright had been cooking the books for a while. A couple of weeks before December's AGM, some £1,400,000 of risky shares had been 'sold' by the L&G to another company that Wright controlled called the Standard Exploration Company (SEC), meaning that these did not appear on the balance sheet at the AGM. The complaint from some shareholders that accounts had not been circulated until the day of the AGM, meaning they couldn't check them, began to appear in a new light. The whole lot was 'sold' back after

L&G failed. Some other liabilities had been transferred to British America Corporation – another Wright company – shortly before this was wound up as insolvent; there were some queries in court as to whether the dates on the paperwork were genuine or had been backdated.

A report issued in December 1901 showed that at the end of September 1900 L&G owed £1,263,000 to BAC and two other Wright companies, meaning that it was 'hopelessly insolvent' and should have stopped trading. Instead, Wright had 'manufactured' assets to make the company look better. Shares had been valued well above their current market price because it was claimed they would do well in the long term (a court was later to hear that shares valued at £2,332,632 were mostly worthless; nearly a quarter of them were in companies like SEC that were equally bankrupt). As well as the £1,400,000 of risky shares moved to SEC, BAC had loaned £200,000 to L&G, laundered through SEC on the way. Two other Wright companies had disposed of their assets without paying any dividends, yet their worthless shares held by L&G were given

a large book value and then sold on to BAC. Wright also tried to raise a large amount by speculating in the shares of a company called Lake View. He borrowed £500,000 from 'a group of gentlemen', later referred to as 'the syndicate', and signed over some of the shares as security. Allegedly the syndicate had agreed not to sell these shares below Wright's target price of £17 but did so, making a large profit and leaving the L&G badly out of pocket. The liquidators ended up suing the syndicate for a million pounds, but lost when it turned out that the £17 figure wasn't documented anywhere.

One other interesting note was that Wright had been bribing the financial press to promote specific companies in their reports; knowing this would happen, he could buy shares beforehand and sell them at a profit afterwards. This was done, not by cash in brown envelopes, but by the reporters buying shares in some of Wright's new companies. As described earlier, new companies would often only demand part of the share price initially and then 'call' the rest of it in tranches over several months. When these companies made such calls,

This monument to Frank Pick, deputy chairman of the London Passenger Transport Board (LPTB) is at Piccadilly Circus station; he is unlikely to have condoned Wright's methods.

MAY AND READ

Two minor characters in this story are Frank Boyd May and E.B. Read, about whom little or nothing is known.

Sometime in 1896, Mr Read approached his friend Frank May to discuss the BS&WR – apparently Mr Read's father had an interest in it. He suggested that May could find someone with the sort of money that would be needed to build the railway. May met with Whitaker Wright on 1 December to discuss this and, on the following day, he presented Wright with an agreement to pay him 2 per cent of the value of the BS&WR's shares that L&G bought, which they both signed. In 1898, after some prevarication requiring May to bring an action in court, the company paid May £35,320 in commission, which he split equally with Read. This was a pretty good deal for the pair, representing about £1.5 million each in 2019 money.

In 1901, May sued for another £26,600, representing 2 per cent of the additional shares created by the 1899 and 1900 Acts of Parliament. He claimed that he had indicated the Paddington, Euston and Elephant extensions as dotted lines on a plan he showed to Wright at their first meeting. However, Mr Justice Bigham decided that the agreement did not extend to anything beyond the original shares and any discussion of the possibility in 1896 was simply to show how good an investment it would be.

What was never explained was what information May and Read had that was worth such a large sum of money.

Wright would mark the reporters as having paid up without a penny actually being handed over.

At the end of 1902, the Attorney-General decided not to prosecute anyone over the L&G collapse. There was a lot of disquiet about this, and over the next few months there were questions asked in Parliament, legal experts argued back and forward in the pages of *The Times*, while a group of shareholders put together a private prosecution. On 10 March 1903, a judge gave permission for this to go ahead and the same day a summons was issued for Wright to appear in court. When this was served at his mansion that evening, his wife stated that he was 'away for the benefit of his health'. Suspecting that he had fled the country, a warrant was issued for his arrest.

It turned out that Wright had left home on 21 February, taking with him £500 in banknotes obtained by a maid who had cashed a cheque at the local bank. There are claims that Wright had hidden in the icehouse of Witley Park for a week, but at this point there was no warrant out for him and Wright himself said that his barrister had advised there was no reason not to travel. He arrived in Paris on 25 February and stayed there for some time. On 5 March, Mrs Wright, who had been observing the legal activity, sent him a telegram reading 'Everything looks bad', to which he replied with instructions including 'Give Florence £500'. This referred to his young niece Florence Browne, who the next day – together with her maid – took the train to Waterloo and thence to Le Havre, arriving at 14:50 on 7 March. There she met Wright and they boarded the steamer *La Lorraine*, which departed that evening.

On Friday 13 March, the police obtained the numbers of the banknotes and inquired about them. On Saturday, the Bank of England reported that £100 note number 75,775 had been cashed in Paris. This led the police to discover the steamer booking, in the names of M and Mlle Andreoni, and they promptly telegraphed the New York police. When the ship arrived the following morning Wright was arrested. At later hearings an attempt was made to make something of these false names, but Wright claimed that it was the name of the agent at the Paris hotel who had booked the tickets (which had been done on 6 March) and he certainly told the purser of *La Lorraine* their real names the day after sailing.

Wright was imprisoned and attempted to get bail; this ended up at the US Supreme Court, which decided that there was no mechanism for someone awaiting extradition to be bailed. On 2 July, it was reported that Wright was 'seriously ill with vertigo' and would not last six months, but five days later he agreed to be voluntarily extradited. He eventually departed on the *Oceanic* (predecessor of the *Titanic* and once the largest ship in the world) on 29 July in the company of two Scotland Yard detectives, arriving on 5 August. Typically, Wright rejected the stateroom he had been given and insisted on a suite.

After hearings in August and September, Wright was committed for trial on twenty-six charges of fraud. This was originally listed for the Old Bailey in October, but was moved to the Law Courts, mostly because it was felt that the case needed a 'special jury' consisting of people who understood

Whitaker Wright (left) and a Scotland Yard detective on arrival at Liverpool. TATLER

years in prison, the maximum for the offence. Some commentators believed that the judge was biased against Wright, but, on the other hand, Bigham and the prosecutor between them had been able to unravel the knots of Wright's tangled activities and make them clear to the jury.

In normal circumstances Wright would have been hauled off to prison, but because the trial was at the Law Courts – which normally dealt with civil cases – instead of the Old Bailey, the process was different. He was locked in a comfortable room with some associates and court officials and enjoyed a whisky and cigar. He pulled out his watch and chain and gave them to a friend, saying 'I shall have no use for these in this place. I give them to you to keep for me.' He started to light another cigar but collapsed. Despite a doctor arriving within a few minutes, he died within a quarter of an hour.

This might have seemed unfortunate, but when a post-mortem was held it turned out that the death was due to cyanide poisoning and that it must have been deliberate. The *Daily Mirror* had a front page explaining how a poison capsule was hidden in a cigar, but the actual evidence did not support that; it was more likely that Wright put it in his mouth during a visit to the toilet and swallowed it a bit later. What was made clear was that, unlike at the Old Bailey, it was not normal to search prisoners at the Law Courts, meaning Wright could easily have brought the cyanide with him in his pockets – it turned out that he was also carrying a loaded revolver throughout the last day of the trial!

In the end, this colourful man – once the talk of London – reached an equally colourful end. He is buried at Witley, where he had always been popular because of the hundreds of local people he employed.

As for the BS&WR, what was to happen to it with its finance lost? Would it fade away, leaving a collection of iron pipes deep below ground to slowly rust away? Or would a white knight appear on his charger to save the day?

business matters, but partly because there was a concern about prejudice after certain statements made in the House of Commons. The actual trial began on Monday 11 January in front of Mr Justice Bigham (the judge in the May and Read case and recognized as an expert in corporate law; the prosecuting barrister was also an expert, having been a stockbroker). There was a lot of complex technical evidence heard. On Tuesday 26 January, the twelfth day of the case, the jury took only an hour to find Wright guilty on twenty-four of the twenty-six counts (the judge having told them to ignore the other two). At 3pm, Wright was sentenced to seven

CHAPTER 4

Saved by Yerkes

The white knight – or at least a rather dingy grey one – had actually already appeared: his name was Charles Tyson Yerkes (pronounced 'Yerr-keys'). Yerkes was the son of a banker in Philadelphia. He entered the grain brokerage business from school and by the age of twenty-two had his own company and a seat on the Philadelphia stock exchange. In the next few years he expanded into banking and then street railways (that is, trams). He made his name by helping to rescue the city's finances after the problems following the US Civil War, enabling the city to sell bonds at full price rather than a deep discount.

However, in 1871 the great Chicago fire caused the collapse first of several local businesses and then the entire US bond market. Yerkes found himself owing the city money that he was unable to pay – he was supposed to be looking after city funds, but was instead using them as collateral for his own trading. This was not an unusual practice at the time, but Yerkes found himself caught out by the crash and his political enemies ensured that he could not borrow money to repay the city. He was prosecuted for embezzling $400,000 (though the real reason may have been his refusal to give the city priority over his other creditors), convicted and sentenced to thirty-three months in prison. Although an attempt to blackmail two politicians into keeping him out of prison failed, Yerkes only served seven months: a deal was struck whereby

he was pardoned in return for publicly denying the statements he had made about the two politicians and which were seen as harmful to the state governor and to Ulysses S. Grant, the US President.

Yerkes spent the next ten years rebuilding his fortune, including repaying all his creditors with interest. In 1881, he divorced his wife and married his mistress, moving first to North Dakota and then the next year to Chicago. There he started out as a stockbroker before moving into gas franchises and then into tramways in 1886. As an example of his technique, he acquired his first line by forming a syndicate that spent around $1.5 million to gain a majority of the shares (2,505 out of 5,000). He then created a new company that issued bonds for $1.5 million; the sale of these paid for the initial purchase cost. The original company then leased everything to the new company, leaving Yerkes and his partners having spent nothing to obtain a company that paid around $250,000 in dividends every year. The Chicago area can be divided roughly into three parts: 'north side', 'west side' and 'south side'. Yerkes managed to get control of the tramways on the north and west sides, but never succeeded with the south side. Despite his own claim that he liked to 'buy up old junk, fix it up a little, and unload it upon other fellows', he actually brought major benefits to his lines. He extended his network by around 800km (500 miles), refitted abandoned tunnels under the Chicago River to eliminate the bottlenecks caused by swing bridges, and converted the lines from horse power first to use cable traction and then electricity. When an elevated railway threatened his monopoly of the west side, he took it over via a secret deal and then extended it to form what is still known as 'the Loop'. The services on the Loop were often crowded, but Yerkes refused to lengthen the trains, famously saying 'The straphangers pay the dividends.'

Though he was not alone in using them, Yerkes was an expert in dubious or dirty tactics. He would routinely bribe city councillors to vote to give him new franchises or renew them for long periods. If a politician couldn't be bought, Yerkes would find a secret that could be used to blackmail him. And if that didn't work, he would create such a secret. The author Theodore Dreiser tells a story of how Cowperwood (*see* Sidebar) needed to corrupt the new mayor. The mayor was asked by a political friend to find a position for a young widow as a stenographer. Before long, witnesses had collected plenty of evidence of the mayor's meetings with the widow (who, unbeknown to him, was actually a prostitute and political spy) at various restaurants and hotels. Soon after this, the young lady returned to Washington DC. The mayor sent her letters, which were added to the evidence being collected by Cowperwood's assistant. When the mayor found himself opposed to Cowperwood, the latter merely needed to mention these letters and a possible breach of promise suit to eliminate the difficulty.

In 1898, as part of the 'Chicago Traction Wars', Yerkes attempted to obtain a fifty-year extension of his franchises. Despite large bribes to the aldermen, alleged to total over a million dollars, public opinion against the extension – partly expressed in the form of mobs threatening the voters – was strong enough that he failed. Rather than fight further, he sold his interests in Chicago transport for $20 million and moved to New York to become a financier and his wife a socialite. Within a few years his holding company, now in other hands, had gone bankrupt.

Yerkes was still interested in public transport and in 1900 he appeared in London, presumably looking for new worlds to conquer (he had also

FRANK COWPERWOOD

Frank Cowperwood is the lead character of the *Trilogy of Desire*, a series of three novels (*The Financier, The Titan* and *The Stoic*) by Theodore Dreiser (all three novels are available for free on the Internet). Cowperwood is the son of a bank clerk in Philadelphia who becomes a major financier in the city. He becomes involved in street railways, but the great Chicago fire triggers a financial panic and Cowperwood is caught defrauding the city. He is sent to prison for four and a quarter years, but pulls strings to be pardoned after thirteen months. He then moves to Chicago where he gets involved in the tramways there, improving the network significantly, but his attempt to get complete control fails. He finally moves to London, where he attempts to take control of the underground railways.

The character of Cowperwood was based on Yerkes. While there are a lot of places where the novels should not be relied upon and their story is not a biography of Yerkes – for example, his private life was sometimes tangled, but, as far as we know, it was not as colourful as Cowperwood's amatory adventures – nevertheless the novels give the reader a good idea of the way that financial businesses and public services were run in the later part of the nineteenth century. Those interested in Yerkes are recommended to read them.

apparently looked at the Metropolitan District in 1896). Unlike Chicago, he did not need to spend his time dealing with corrupt politicians: there were railways there that he could simply buy. The Charing Cross, Euston and Hampstead Railway was sitting there unable to raise capital, so a Yerkes syndicate bought it out on 28 September that year, paying £40,000 for the work done so far and £60,000 for the parliamentary deposit. On 15 July 1901, he formed the Metropolitan District Electric Traction Co. Ltd, capitalized at a million pounds. Yerkes held just under a quarter of the shares and most of the rest were held by US financiers; a mere 6.5 per cent or so were sold in London. A month or so earlier, Yerkes had bought a majority of the Metropolitan District's shares for £152,179 and promptly sold them on to the Traction company for the same price, plus 5 per cent per annum interest. This deal also got him another unbuilt line called the Brompton and Piccadilly Circus Railway (B&PCR). In November of the same year the Traction paid £131,016 for the Great Northern and Strand Railway (which, together with the B&PCR, would form the backbone of today's Piccadilly Line) and bought Yerkes's Hampstead line shares off him.

That left one unfinished line: the BS&WR. As we saw earlier, Yerkes's name had already been mentioned in this context, but this time it was for real. In December the Official Receiver started negotiating with Yerkes and on 7 March 1902 agreement was reached: the company would cost the Traction £335,000, paid in cash. This might seem a lot compared with the other lines he had bought, but the company had a parliamentary deposit of £107,000 and there were another £50,000 of BS&WR shares being used to guarantee that the work would be done. When these could eventually be sold, the BS&WR would have actually cost £178,000.

These lines between them (including electrifying the Metropolitan District) meant spending around £16 million, far more than the Traction had. Yerkes started another of his complex financial schemes, this time working with the international banker Edgar Speyer, based in London, and the Old Colony Trust of Boston (USA, not Lincolnshire). Between them, they formed the Underground Electric Railways Company of London (UERL),

capitalized at £5 million, which bought out the Traction's shares at face value. Instead of a normal share issue, Yerkes also invented something called 'certificates', by which shareholders would get the first 5 per cent of profits, certificate holders the next 3 per cent, and the rest would be split equally. As well as the shares and certificates that came from selling his Traction shares, Yerkes also ended up with over a million pounds worth of certificates, while Speyer Brothers and the Old Colony Trust pocketed £250,000 in cash. Like the Traction, UERL was mostly American-owned, though nearly a third was held by British shareholders. Yerkes himself held nearly 10 per cent of the shares.

Construction Continues

In the first half of 1901 the company had spent £276,850, over half of which was on buying land, notably the site of the depot. No dividends could be paid because there was no money to spare, but the promised interest continued to accrue, waiting

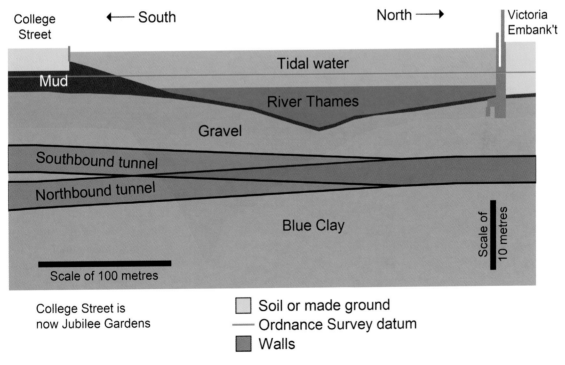

Geology of the Bakerloo crossing the River Thames. BASED ON WILLIAM COPPERTHWAITE

to be paid once some cash came in. The second river tunnel was being dug. Like the first, this went through a section of gravel and the work had to be done in compressed air at up to 35psi (240kPa) to push back the water. Various techniques were used to keep the air in, notably pushing wet clay into holes in front of the shield so that there was a hopefully airtight seal around the front edge of the shield. Nevertheless, air sometimes escaped and could burst through the river bed to cause water-spouts up to 3ft (90cm) high. One such upset a boat in a race, requiring the company to pay damages.

With money now secure, construction could continue, though only on the original part of the line and the connection to the depot. Several Greathead shields were in use at the same time. Though exact details are not available, a typical working team on a running tunnel shield would consist of a ganger in charge, four miners digging out at the workface and four labourers to assist them, another four labourers assembling the rings and doing other work such as building a temporary floor, plus a boy to work in small spaces and do assorted odd jobs. Hourly pay rates were normally 12d, 9d, 7½d, 7d, and 4d, respectively, plus a bonus for each week that exceeded an agreed rate of progress (typically forty-five rings a week). Shifts were normally ten hours. This team was responsible for getting the rings from, and the spoil to, the contractor's narrow-gauge railway, which typically started 10 yards (10m) or so behind the shield and had a gauge of about 12in (30cm). Traditionally, the wagons on this line were hauled by pit ponies, requiring one driver, a brakesman and a team of ponies for each 300yd (270m) of tunnel, but the BS&WR took advantage of new technology and instead used small electric locomotives powered from temporary overhead wires. Similarly, the hand screws used on earlier lines were replaced by hydraulic rams – eight in running tunnels and twenty-two in stations. Overall progress was about forty-four rings per week, a distance of 73ft 4in (just under 22.4m) when in free air; compressed air reduced this by 30–50 per cent.

By the start of 1902, the line was 'largely complete' as far north as Oxford Circus. One side-effect

THE COST OF REMOVING SPOIL

Large amounts of spoil need to be removed from tunnels – the running tunnels between Baker Street and Waterloo alone represent almost 90,000m³ (3 million cu ft), without considering the larger station tunnels and connecting passageways. Perry & Co., the main contractors, hired a firm of carters to take the spoil away from the Oxford Circus and Piccadilly Circus shafts, paying them 3s 10d per load. At the time the contract was made, they estimated that 53,000cu yd (40,500m³) of material would be involved.

However, when the sections of tunnel from these locations joined up with those being dug from the river shaft, Perry & Co. realized that it could use the latter to remove material from these northern sections at a significantly lower cost. The carters sued for their losses, but the court decided that the amount was only an estimate, not a guarantee, and Perry & Co. was entitled to change its plans.

of the grouping into the UERL was that the line no longer needed its own power station; it would simply buy power from the UERL's generating station at Lots Road (near Chelsea). The freed-up space would be used to extend the depot.

By March 1903, the running tunnels were 80 per cent complete and all the station tunnels bar one had been dug. The northbound tunnel was finished in August of the same year, the southbound following it in November. The next step was to build the platforms within the wider tunnels that had been dug for the stations. Work on the depot also started in 1903. The access tunnel was several metres below street level at this point, meaning that the entire site had to be dug out down to the same level. This was a long job: two years later, a third of the area was still unexcavated, though track had already been laid in the completed part, and it was only finished just before the line opened.

Though work was in progress, money was still tight at the UERL. Tube shares weren't selling – the two operating tube lines were not paying good dividends – so Yerkes came up with another complex financial scheme that netted another £7 million. The next year he mortgaged the power station for £775,000 and in 1905 he managed to raise another £2.5 million. The total raised was almost enough to finish the three tube lines and electrify the District, after which, everyone hoped, money would start

'The Elephant' – Lots Road power station on opening in 1905.

rolling in to repay the various loans and reward the shareholders.

Another event in 1903 was yet another Act of Parliament. Its main purpose was to allow the BS&WR to be sold to the Great Northern, Piccadilly and Brompton Railway (an amalgamation of the two Piccadilly Line companies), but Parliament rejected this. The rump of the Bill, allowing purchase of some land at Lambeth, plus a second one to extend the time for completion, gained Royal Assent on 11 August.

In 1904, the company came back with a more adventurous Bill, allowing the construction of three new stations at Edgware Road, Lambeth North and Regent's Park, the last of these attempting to overturn the previous ban on a station between Oxford Circus and Baker Street. The Bill also asked to increase the company's capital by another £440,000, though dissent by the London County Council reduced this to £384,000. With this change, it went through without difficulty, gaining Royal Assent on 22 July. The money was needed partly for the new stations, but also to pay increased costs because of the Couronnes disaster in Paris. On 10 August 1903, a fire on a train on what is now Line 2 of the Paris metro resulted in the deaths of eighty-four people, mostly at Couronnes station. In May 1904, the Board of Trade issued a number of new requirements for underground lines, such as forbidding the use of woodwork for station platforms. All these changes, of course, cost money, but the Yerkes companies were quick to implement them, building concrete platforms and steel trains. Somewhere around this time, the Board of Trade objected to the design of Oxford Circus station, meaning that it had to undergo major redesign and rebuilding before it even opened.

By early 1905, the trains themselves were on order. Track was being laid in the tunnels and lifts were being installed in the stations, often in the shafts originally used to reach tunnel level and start the original digging. By October, the track and depot were ready for use, while tiling the stations and constructing the electricity substations were both not far behind. The first test train ran in November between the depot and Baker Street and very soon test trains were running regularly.

In November, Yerkes returned to New York City for a visit; while there, he suffered another attack of nephritis (then known as 'Bright's disease'). On 29 December, only ten weeks before the line finally opened, Charles Tyson Yerkes died at the age of sixty-eight. He left an estate of $4 million, a third of it to his estranged wife, houses and an art collection large enough to require a separate mansion to hold it. He also left London three tube lines that would otherwise probably not have come into existence for many years, if ever.

YERKES ON THE MOON

If you look up at the full moon on a clear night, near the right-hand edge you will see the dark area called the Mare Crisium ('Sea of Crises'). At about the 8 o'clock position, though not visible with the naked eye, is the impact crater Yerkes with its two satellite craters 'Yerkes E' and 'Yerkes V'. But why is there a crater named after a rather dubious financier?

Like many rich men of the nineteenth century, Yerkes was a philanthropist and an art collector. In 1892, he was having problems with his public reputation when he was approached by Professor Hale of the University of Chicago, who wanted a new telescope (plus observatory to hold it) and suggested that funding this would greatly enhance Yerkes's image. Though originally he only intended to pay for the telescope, Yerkes eventually footed the bill for the entire observatory – the tale is told that Hale leaked a story to the press that Yerkes had offered the whole cost and the latter realized he had been outmanoeuvred. The Yerkes Observatory was opened in 1897 and the telescope, with its 40in (102cm) lens, is still the largest refracting telescope in the world. (Dreiser also mentions the telescope: Cowperwood first gained an interest in astronomy by watching the stars from the garden of his prison cell.) Unlike many other craters in the area, Yerkes is almost filled with lava and as a result is very difficult to distinguish.

Mare Crisium taken from the NASA Lunar Reconnaissance Orbiter. Yerkes is near the left edge with Yerkes E connected to it by a ridge; Yerkes V is the small dot below Yerkes E. NASA

CHAPTER 5

The Bakerloo Opens

Service Commences

On Saturday 10 March 1906, the BS&WR opened for business from Lambeth North to Baker Street. The week leading up to the opening was a busy one for the railway, which ran a full 'dress rehearsal'. The whole service was operated as if the line was open. At the station entrances, booking clerks practised issuing tickets and the liftmen worked their lifts up and down the shafts all day. At tunnel level, a full timetable of trains was operated. The train crews would open and close the train doors (or, rather, gates), estimating how long it would take for the non-existent passengers to board or alight, and announced each station in a loud voice to the empty carriages. On the Wednesday, the press was allowed to ride one of these trains, starting at the depot and alighting at Baker Street, where they were given a good lunch, speeches by the directors and hand-outs to ease the job of writing their 'copy' (this is the first sighting of the 'created by cricket enthusiasts' story).

The formal opening on the Saturday was carried out by the chairman of the London County Council; over 200 of the great and good rode from Trafalgar Square to Lambeth North, then back to Baker Street, before partaking in the traditional railway opening banquet. 37,000 people rode the line on the first day. The line only operated a single class

of accommodation, making the businessman and society lady mix with the working man. Initially there was a flat fare of 2d for all journeys (and twenty-five tickets could be bought for the price of twenty-four). Cheap single and return tickets for workmen (usually half the normal price) were also sold before 08:00.

Right from day one, the line ran an intensive service. There were 20tph (trains per hour each way) between 07:30 and 23:30, with 12tph for two hours in the early morning and 10tph for the last hour at night. Sunday service started at 07:30 at 10tph, before increasing to 20tph at 11:00 for the rest of the day. However, the trains only ran at an average speed of 26km/h (16mph). The actual reason for this was the restricted power of the motors that would fit in the trains, but Yerkes's engineer James Chapman cheekily told Parliament that the human frame could not withstand anything quicker in a tube: 'A passenger cannot be handled like a bullet in a gun.' The trains themselves are discussed in Chapter 12.

At the northern end there were no reversing facilities at Baker Street, partly because the platforms were at different levels. Therefore trains continued to the incomplete Marylebone station, where they reversed over a crossover just east of the station; a temporary signal box was suspended over the tracks in the crossover tunnel.

Lambeth North station – the original southern terminus – as it is today.

The Route

On leaving Elephant & Castle station, which was to open on 5 August, the line runs under London Road to St George's Circus, where it turns left into Westminster Bridge Road. It follows that through Lambeth North station and past the junction with the link to London Road depot, until it crosses the intersection with Upper Marsh and Lower Marsh and turns to run under the erstwhile Eurostar platforms of Waterloo main-line station (at the time this area was occupied by a goods depot). Its own Waterloo station is on a sharp left-hand curve centred roughly where the line crosses York Road.

Though the line now runs under the Shell Centre and Jubilee Gardens, at the time the curve was necessary to get the line into Vine Street and then College Street. These streets were so narrow that the tunnels needed to be stacked one above the other (the southbound on top) in order to stay

This folly and its sibling in Crescent Gardens are actually covers for air shafts down into Regent's Park station.

under them and this explains why the platforms at Waterloo are at different levels. Once under the river (which was wider then, before the South Bank was built), the two tunnels could resume the same level, though it took most of the river to do so.

The route under the river is at a diagonal so as to meet Northumberland Avenue, with Embankment station under the road junctions. From there, it runs straight up to Trafalgar Square, with the station under Cockspur Street from the statue of Charles I to just past Spring Gardens. It then follows Haymarket before making a graceful turn across Piccadilly Circus (with the station underneath) and into Regent Street. At Oxford Circus the platforms are almost entirely north of Oxford Street and stretch to Margaret Street. The tunnels then follow the road's S-bend into Portland Place.

At the north end of Portland Place the line continues straight, running under the middle of Crescent Gardens. Regent's Park station lies under these gardens, meaning that access is along a long passageway from Marylebone Road. Once across the road and clear of the platforms, the line takes a gentle left turn under Park Street Gardens and across the

Outer Circle (not an Underground line but another road), before straightening out about 65m (roughly 210ft) north of the latter. After passing under the end of the boating lake, it shifts slightly southwards to run through Baker Street station, with the southbound platform underneath the northbound, and into line with Melcombe Street (then New Street) to continue to Marylebone station. In doing so, 30 Allsop Place and 12 Cornwall Terrace – plus their neighbours – are the only places where the line runs under private houses.

London Road depot occupies a rough trapezium bounded by London Road, Lambeth Road, Gladstone Street and a short length of St George's Road. It is sited well below ground level, because this was the only practical way to provide an access track. By modern standards it is cramped: it is about big enough for seventy-five cars, but had to handle well over one hundred. Originally the depot contained three train sheds, but only one of them remains; there have also been minor changes to the track layout over the years. Because the line did not emerge on the surface anywhere, a ramp was built to allow trains to be brought to the site

London Road depot today; the train hiding in the corner is 1967 Stock unit 3067, used for training cleaners.

by road. The connecting line starts at the western corner of the site, where it disappears under the road junction. Though there are two tracks entering the tunnel, only the southern one is the actual connection; the other is a headshunt to allow trains to shunt between depot tracks. The link line meets the running tunnels where St George's Road merges into Westminster Bridge Road, but the actual junction is just west of Bayliss Road (then Oakley Street), where the main tracks are converging after Lambeth North station.

In addition, the original running tunnels actually started east of Elephant & Castle, extending along the New Kent Road to just west of the main-line railway bridge. This extension provided storage sidings for trains until it was destroyed in the 1930s.

Working to Standards

The Yerkes group was building three tube lines at once and imposed common standards where it could. The running tunnels normally had a diameter of 11ft 8¼in (3,562mm), though this would widen to as much as 12ft 6in (3,810mm) on curves, while the station tunnels were 21ft 2½in (6,464mm). The other Yerkes lines were to have station platforms 350ft (107m) long, but enough work had already been done on the Bakerloo before it was taken over that it had to settle for a length of 291ft (89m). To avoid fire risk, the platforms were concrete with stone edging. While some tube lines have tunnels that climb into each station to aid braking and then descend on departure to improve acceleration, the general climb of the Bakerloo northwards from the Thames made that impractical. Another situation where the Bakerloo did things differently was the rails themselves: the Yerkes standard was to have the rails about 45ft (13.7m) long, but getting the rails down vertical shafts and then rotated into the tunnels became a major geometry problem that resulted in imposing a limit of 36ft 5in (11.1m).

The architect Leslie Green was engaged to design the stations on all three Yerkes tubes. He came up with a consistent design for both the exteriors and interiors that made them instantly recognizable to the public and formed the first step towards creating a unified brand for the UERL. On the Bakerloo he designed all eleven of the stations from Elephant & Castle to Edgware Road. Where there was a surface building, it was two stories with a structural steel frame that created wide open spaces inside and made it practical to build on top later. Columns broke up the frontage into large bays, which could be entrances, exits, or even retail premises, while each bay had a semicircular window above it. The whole exterior was tiled in a dark 'oxblood' red that was distinctive and easy to spot from a distance without being garish – the appearance is so memorable that the BBC recreated it for the soap opera *EastEnders*. The horizontal between the two floors bore the name of the station, though this has been removed from two of the four remaining examples on the Bakerloo, while the name of the company was immediately under the roofline; no examples of this latter feature survive, though Holloway Road on the Piccadilly Line has 'G N P & B Ry' beside the name.

Not every station had the Green exterior. Waterloo was far enough advanced that no attempt was made to retrofit it. Embankment station did not have its own building (nor, for that matter, lifts); instead, there was a long sloping tunnel from the eastbound platform of the existing District station and then stairs. Finally, Trafalgar Square and Regent's Park had no surface buildings at all, though the latter was entered through two parallel subways in a dramatic dark green somewhat spoiled by modern handrails. The buildings at Piccadilly Circus, Baker Street and Marylebone have all subsequently been demolished.

The same consistency was found inside the buildings. The entrance and exit would normally be tiled in white with one or more horizontal green lines. Often there were other decorative features, such as the lifts at Regent's Park or the ticket windows at Edgware Road. At platform level the original idea was to have plain white tiling so as to maximize the use of the available lighting, but

The Bakerloo end of the original passageway from the District platforms at Embankment.

Yerkes – who was interested in art – intervened and demanded something more. The end result was a combination of consistency with uniqueness. The platform tunnels were tiled for the first 2–2.5m (6ft 6in–8ft) with white plaster above that, except that there were stripes of tiles right across the tunnels forming an impression of rings; double rings indicated something significant like an exit. On the side wall, the station name would be designed into the tiling, while the remaining space was taken up with a regular pattern that was unique to each

Re-creation of the Leslie Green tile pattern at Lambeth North.

station on the three lines. This made the stations easier to identify: a regular traveller would soon learn the patterns at their stations and could spot them even if they couldn't see or read the name. Regrettably, few of these original designs survive on the Bakerloo, having fallen prey to later changes of 'house style'; in at least one case what is there now is actually a modern re-creation. Trafalgar Square was unique in that only the southbound platform got the Green treatment; the northbound was plain white.

Surface and platform were normally connected by two or three vertical shafts. One of these would be 18ft (5.5m) in diameter and contain a spiral staircase, while the remainder would be 23ft (7m) and each hold two Otis lifts, each of which could carry seventy passengers plus the operator. An alternative arrangement used a 30ft (9.1m) shaft holding three lifts. Normally, the lifts would not descend all the way to platform level but, rather, to an intermediate landing typically 15ft (4.5m) above. At Trafalgar Square and Regent's Park the lack of station buildings meant that the lift equipment had to be underneath the lifts rather than on top, presumably with the lift cables running up the shaft and over a pulley at the top. The lifts typically oper-

ated at 100ft/sec (30m/s), though they could achieve twice that. The Bakerloo ended up with thirty-five lifts; a change of mind from the original design meant that sometimes a lift was omitted from a shaft. The Bakerloo was also the first London tube line with ventilation designed in: fans sucked air out of the tunnels and through ducts in the shafts to an exhaust on the roof, while fresh air was drawn down the shafts to replace it.

There were three stations where the Bakerloo met other tube lines. At Elephant & Castle and Oxford Circus the two companies maintained separate stations and, at least initially, required changing passengers to buy a second ticket, but both stations had connecting passages at platform level (presumably with ticket checkers somewhere along them). Piccadilly Circus, on the other hand, was the one station on the Bakerloo that served another Yerkes tube. There was a single surface station, though with separate banks of lifts to each line, as well as the expected connecting passages. All stations on both lines could issue tickets to any station on the other line, making it much easier for passengers.

All three Yerkes lines were electrified on the same scheme as the Metropolitan and District had been: a positive current rail outside the running rails and a negative between them, though for reasons explained later the Bakerloo initially had the positive and negative reversed. The supply was at 600V DC, split 2:1 so that the outside rail was at +400V relative to earth and the central one at −200V. The power was fed at high voltage from Lots Road to a substation at Embankment and thence to two others at Baker Street and London Road.

The Early Years

The Bakerloo was very popular on its opening day, but after this the traffic was disappointing – for example, in April a rush-hour train was noted by the press as carrying fewer than ninety passengers. Trains were supposed to have six cars in the peaks and three at other times, but they were shortened to three and two and the service cut by a third in order to save money: a six-car train required a driver, a conductor and four gatemen. But over the next few months demand picked up, allowing the full service level to be restored. In early November, the weekly takings overtook the calendar, reaching £2,105, double what they had been in July. Some longer trains were introduced the following March and at the end of December there were 27tph in the peaks and 17tph the rest of the time. At the start of 1908 the line returned to universal three-car trains. In October, the service increased again, to 35tph and 20tph respectively (the former exceeding today's busiest routes), and the last northbound train left Piccadilly Circus at 1:00 on weekdays. Nevertheless, traffic did not reach the predictions of over 30 million passengers a year seen in the 1900 prospectus: in 1906, it carried just under 9.8 million, increasing to 20.5 million the following (full) year and 28.2 million in 1909.

One thing blamed for insufficient demand was the 2d flat fare. Tickets were collected at the beginning of the journey and there were concerns that people were slipping past distracted collectors without paying, so that was changed to collecting at the exit. But much more significant was that it was seen as overly expensive for short journeys, so a few

months after opening it was changed to a distance-based system of 1d per mile in ½d steps. The UERL also decided to introduce through fares, starting on 12 November 1906 with journeys between the Bakerloo and the District, but extending to include the Piccadilly and Hampstead lines when they opened. The scheme also covered the London United Tramways, which Yerkes had taken control of in 1902 and merged into the UERL. Season tickets were introduced on 1 November, but abolished less than two years later except for journeys to the District, only to be reinstated in 1911. From 1908 to 1916, it was possible to buy strips of six tickets at a slight discount: nothing for penny tickets; 1d for up to 2½d tickets; 2d for 3d and 3½d tickets; and 3d for 4d and 5d tickets. *The Times* noted that the informal motto of the tubes was 'no waiting' and the strips eliminated the last cause of delay – booking office queues.

In contrast to all these savings, in late 1907 a meeting about price competition between the various transport companies in London led to fare rises all round, albeit only ½d or 1d. The UERL was in money trouble again, as one of Yerkes's complex financial instruments needed to be paid off in 1908 and another scheme needed to be devised to find the money. But, with the help of some loans from Speyer Brothers, it survived. The increased traffic meant that some modest dividends could finally be paid: 1.5 per cent in 1909 and 2 per cent in the first half of 1910. These were not great amounts and certainly nowhere near enough to encourage people to buy the shares – the money was mostly going into the UERL's coffers – but at least it was a start. One result of actual profits was that some fares were cut again and it now cost only 2d to go from Edgware Road all the way to Waterloo.

On 5 August 1906, Elephant & Castle station opened, providing a connection with the C&SLR and another main-line railway. Much more importantly, however, was the extension at the other end. Marylebone station was already well advanced – as we've already seen, trains were reversing there – and on 27 March 1907 it opened for service. It had been built to serve the Great Central Railway

Elephant & Castle Bakerloo entrance, with a sympathetic building added on top.

station (indeed, the initial name of the station was 'Great Central') and this showed. The station was on the corner of the erstwhile Harewood Square, which had disappeared under the new station, with the tunnels forming a diagonal under private prop-

erty to link Melcombe Place on the east with Bell Street (then partly Great James Street) on the west. Although there was a station building on top of the lift shaft, passengers were expected to reach the station by a subway under the road to the main-line

Edgware Road station.

station; the ticket office and lift entrances were at the Bakerloo end of the subway, not at ground level. Being only a single storey whose visible purpose was just to protect the stairs down from the rain, the station appearance was non-standard, though it did have some elements of the Leslie Green style, including the oxblood tiles. For the first couple of months only one platform was in use, but on 12 May the reversing move shifted west, along the tunnels under Bell Street, to Edgware Road station in order to start test running.

Edgware Road opened just over a month later, on 15 June. It sits at the west end of Bell Street, where it terminates at the eponymous Roman thoroughfare, a short walk from the east end of the Paddington canal basin. Today it lies in the shadow of the Marylebone Flyover (the start of the Westway and one of the few legacies of the 1960s 'Ringway' scheme to cover London with motorways). The station is a typical example of Green's work, though like Elephant one wall is now covered by a strange vertical shrubbery. Today the upper storey contains assorted businesses under the address 'Bakerloo Chambers'.

TWO EDGWARE ROAD STATIONS

Travellers in London are sometimes confused by the fact that there are two Edgware Road stations on the Underground map. Why? New Yorkers may cope with five stations in a line called 23rd Street, but Londoners want more precision.

The stations are not very far apart: it's only a 210m (230 yards) walk between their entrances. Edgware Road is also an obvious name, given the importance of the road to London through the ages. It is also not the only place where two stations were built in close proximity by two different companies and given the same name – at one time there were three New Cross stations in a row along the New Cross Road. However, in most of these cases the stations formed a convenient interchange between lines and were (whether initially or later) linked up into a single one.

The two Edgware Roads, though, are not worth connecting together. There are interchanges immediately to either side, but the Bakerloo station sees enough business that there is no point making people change trains just to increase the crowds at the Circle Line station. But why not rename one of them? At Shepherd's Bush one of the two stations gained a 'Market' suffix; after all, it's right by one. One of the New Crosses became New Cross Gate when the owning companies merged (the third one had closed long before). Elsewhere, Tottenham Court Road became Goodge Street so that Oxford Street could merge with the other Tottenham Court Road.

But at Edgware Road nobody has ever managed to come up with a good name that's worth the cost of making the change; the most recent published proposal was 'Church Street Market' in 2007. Meanwhile, the namesakes remain.

The Arrival of Albert Henry Stanley

Yerkes' death just before opening left a huge hole at the top of the UERL. He had combined financial wizardry with railway operating experience; finding another like him would be impossible. So the board split the job: for chairman, they appointed Edgar Speyer, who, after all, had come up with much of the money in the first place. For managing director and deputy chairman, however, Speyer himself went north to poach Sir George Gibb, general manager of the North Eastern Railway, one of the biggest – and richest – railways in the country. People wondered why Gibb would jump from this to 'a few miles of electric lines', but the reason was in fact obvious. At the NER Gibb earned £5,000 a year and the board had refused him a 20 per cent raise, but on the UERL he started at £8,000 with a plan to raise that to £10,000. In addition, he got a 'golden handshake' of another £10,000 to compensate for the loss of his NER pension.

Gibb, in turn, saw the need for a general manager and the board wanted to placate the mostly American shareholders, who felt that Englishmen just didn't have that 'get up and go' that was needed to fix the UERL's financial problems. The thirty-two-year-old English-born manager of the New Jersey tramway system was persuaded, perhaps with the help of the Old Colony Trust of Boston, to come to London to try his hand. And so one Albert Henry Stanley entered the scene. His arrival was to change London's transport forever.

Initially the different tube lines organized their own publicity. Posters for the Bakerloo emphasized the number of different connections and many were sold as postcards. But Stanley could see that much more was wanted. Shortly after arriving, he borrowed the huge sum of £50,000 to pay for newspaper advertising, only to discover that the newspapers were happy to print news stories about the railways for free, leaving the money unspent. But his true coup de grace was to convince all the underground railways, including the three independent tubes and the Metropolitan, to come together under one common title: the UNDERGROUND.

This new name came into use at the start of 1908. The style was very specific: the letters were white on light blue with thin lines between the letters. Usually the smaller letters had a bar above and below, or, on vertical signs, to each side. The

Maida Vale showing the UNDERGROUND logo in both original and circle-and-bar forms.

individual companies were asked to eliminate their own names in normal use (obviously they would remain on legal documents), though this met with varying success. Stanley also declared war on the word 'tube', though he never managed to completely conquer it. As part of the same campaign a standard map was produced that could be displayed at stations and also, as a folded card, handed out by the millions to users of the system. Strip maps were added above the windows in the trains for the first time. Other publicity included an Underground-themed board game something like Snakes and Ladders, with squares carrying penalties or bonuses. And, to encourage the public view of this new unity, through bookings were extended to cover most of the network.

It was later that year, though, that an unknown person managed to come up with the iconic symbol that would represent the underground lines and, eventually, all public transport in London: the circle-and-bar. Initially this was only used to carry station names and until 1916 the circle was solid, but it had arrived and it would stay.

Traffic continued to increase and there were complaints about overcrowding on the trains in letters to *The Times*. A correspondent on 5 February 1909 spotted no less than seventeen straphangers in his carriage and told of a person who couldn't fight through them in time to get out at Regent's Park. The conductor responded by telling him off for sitting so far from the car ends (where the exits were). Two weeks later it appeared that the staff had 'solved' this by preventing people getting on to overcrowded trains, but of course this was no more popular.

Unity and Changes

In 1910, the unity of the tube lines was finally realized legally. The Piccadilly company was renamed London Electric Railways (LER) and absorbed the other two, meaning that the BS&WR ceased to exist; from now on it was the LER Bakerloo Line. In order to get the required legislation through, the LER had to agree to changes in workmen's tickets: single tickets were eliminated, but returns became available between any two stations irrespective of which of the three lines they were on. The name of the BS&WR and its siblings quickly disappeared from station rooflines, to be replaced by plain tiles or, in some cases, the station's name in black on white tiles. The next year the UERL merged with the London General Omnibus Company, which ran the vast majority of bus services in London; for many years thereafter the profitable buses would help prop up the UERL's finances. Finally, on 1 January 1913, two of the three independent tube lines – the C&SLR and the Central London Railway – were absorbed into what was becoming known as 'The Combine'. (The Great Northern and City Railway was bought out by the Metropolitan Railway.)

Post-amalgamation stock no longer carried individual company names.
LURS COLLECTION 06813

ELECTRICAL PROBLEMS

The London Underground is almost unique in having electric trains that use positive and negative power rails, rather than utilizing the running rails as one half of the circuit. (Line 1 in Milan also uses this system; it originated in the USA, where it was once popular.) This system was introduced when the Inner Circle was electrified and was used for all of the Yerkes tubes from the beginning. The other early lines were eventually converted to it as well.

The advantage of the four-rail system was that it was easier to isolate the power from anything else, particularly considering that the lines were running in metal tubes. Solid china or ceramic insulators could be used since they only had to bear the weight of the rail, not the whole weight of a loaded train. If the return was through the running rails leakage could cause corrosion of water pipes and interfere with telephone wires. The running rails were also used for track circuits (see Chapter 13) and stray traction current was unwelcome.

However, during test running on the Bakerloo it became clear that there was leakage between the positive rail, on the outside, and the tunnel itself. The other Yerkes tubes did not have this problem because the bottom 2ft (60cm) of the tube was lined with concrete. This leakage would not have been a problem in itself, but the Embankment substation also supplied the District and this was having problems with leakage from the *negative* rail. The solution adopted just before opening was to reverse the polarity on the Bakerloo, putting the positive rail in the centre.

While there was no connection to any other line, this was just a quirk of the Bakerloo. But when such connections were eventually made it would become an issue. By 1917, the power supplies had been broken into sections that could be controlled more precisely and the Bakerloo's current rails reverted to the standard arrangement.

Three stations underwent significant changes during this period. In 1911, the Hampstead line gained powers to extend to Embankment. With two tube lines to serve, the current arrangements were clearly insufficient. A new circulating area was scooped out under the District Line platforms and from it two escalators descended to just above the Bakerloo platforms, with stairs down. There was also a long new passage to the Hampstead line with a green ring motif, while the original access passage was closed to the public. This new arrangement opened to Bakerloo passengers on 2 March 1914, though the Hampstead service had to wait another thirty-five days. (These were not actually the first escalators on the Bakerloo, having missed that achievement by a smidgeon over three months. We will see which station pipped them to the post in the next chapter.)

The second station to be rebuilt was Oxford Circus. From the opening of the Bakerloo there were two stations on the surface, facing each other sullenly from either side of Argyll Street. Since the Bakerloo and Central crossed at right angles there

Low-level connecting passage at Embankment, showing both the original design and recent posters.

The circulating area for the tube lines, under the surface platforms at Baker Street.

was plenty of demand for transfers; in 1909, almost 2½ million passengers did so. At the same time, the 3 million Bakerloo passengers had outgrown the facilities of the station and radical surgery was needed. A new booking hall was built in the basement of the Bakerloo station and two escalators linked it to a lower circulating area from which passengers could reach either line. The three Bakerloo lifts were removed: anyone who wanted one could use the Central's lifts and the connecting passageways. These facilities came into use on 9 May 1914.

Finally, at Baker Street a new circulating area was dug out beneath the four Metropolitan Line 'main line' platforms, connected to them by staircases. Two more escalators were then installed in a new shaft down to tube level, though the lifts to the surface remained in place. This facility opened on 15 October 1914.

However, despite all this progress, there was one obvious problem with the Bakerloo.

CHAPTER 6

Extending the Line

Paddington

To anyone looking at a map, there was a clear and obvious problem with the Bakerloo in its early days. Although Edgware Road station was less than 800m (half a mile) from Paddington, headquarters of the Great Western Railway and thus gateway to a swathe of the country stretching from London to cover half of Wales and most of southwest England, passengers wanting to get there from the West End or Southwark needed to change at Baker Street on to the Metropolitan. Those coming off the Great Central at Marylebone were even worse off: they either had to backtrack via Baker Street and pay extra for the 'privilege', or they found themselves walking further than the Bakerloo would carry them. Clearly the Bakerloo should go to Paddington (though the Metropolitan were less than happy about the idea of competition along this axis), so why hadn't it?

One reason it hadn't was because it was not clear where the line should go after Paddington. Yerkes had always been enthusiastic about extending into open countryside, or at least the suburbs, to attract new custom (provided, of course, that it was his railways that were doing the extending). Given that the line was heading west, the obvious direction was anywhere in an arc from the Thames to the Edgware Road, though the latter was perhaps

better assigned to the Hampstead line. But this wasn't a foregone conclusion: what about heading for Chelsea or a second route to Chiswick?

The BS&WR's 1900 Act would put their Paddington station near the west end of the GWR one, with a connecting subway and the line facing roughly westwards. From there, it was clear that extending slightly north of west would take the line between the railway and the canal to serve the areas of Westbourne Green and Kensal New Town before crossing under the cemetery to reach Willesden Junction on the London and North Western Railway (LNWR). This was a reasonable plan, but, as we've seen, there was no money to fund it.

The 1906 Act took a completely different approach (literally). This time the station would lie under London Street, underneath and perpendicular to the Inner Circle one, with the tunnels extending as far as the junction with Grand Junction Road (now Sussex Gardens). This had the advantage of putting the passengers at the concourse end of the GWR station rather than the country end, but would be expensive because the route involved a more than 90-degree turn under private property and would scupper the obvious extension plans because it left the line heading for Hyde Park Corner, mostly under the park itself. While a future 180-degree turn could be added to bring it back in the 'right' direction, that would result in an S-bend

Would Yerkes have viewed Watford as a tempting target or a step too far? A southbound 'Borrowed Stock' train approaches Watford High Street. LURS COLLECTION 01414

that was almost twice as long as necessary. The advantage, though, was that it did not threaten the GWR, which instead would be beneficiaries from the plan.

In 1908, another player entered the scene. Back in 1898 a company called the North West London Railway (NWLR) had proposed a tube line running under the Edgware Road in an almost straight line from Marble Arch at one end to Cricklewood at the other. The first of five intermediate stations would be at almost the same place that the BS&WR would suggest for its Edgware Road station, while two others, as well as both termini, would offer easy interchange with railways. The Bill went through Parliament with little debate and received Royal Assent on 9 August 1899. However, another depressed money market – in this case caused by the start of the second Boer War – and a lack of results from tube lines so far meant that no work was actually done. In 1906, a second Act extended the line southwards to Victoria, terminating under what is now the Apollo Victoria Theatre, with an intermediate station at Hyde Park Corner (thus interchanging with the Piccadilly Line). The additional length (and costs) did not alter the lack of activity.

In 1908, however, the NWLR came back to Parliament a third time, now with a radical change.

The Bill proposed a 827yd (756m) connection between the Bakerloo and NWLR at Edgware Road, with the latter abandoned south of there. The BS&WR would build and run the NWLR in exchange for a quarter of the gross receipts. The main route of the combined line would therefore be Elephant & Castle to Cricklewood, though the Bakerloo preferred to cut it back to Brondesbury, at the Metropolitan's Kilburn station. The extension to Paddington, for which the Bakerloo still had powers, would be run as a shuttle service to Edgware Road with passengers required to change trains there; the Paddington and Cricklewood branches would have had separate platforms.

Just about everybody disliked this proposal. The Metropolitan saw it as direct competition to their services between Kilburn and Baker Street. The GWR were insulted by being relegated to a branch line and, to double the insult, were being asked to pay much of the cost of building that branch. Middlesex County Council had supported the idea when it extended to Cricklewood where their tramways started, but were less enthusiastic when a gap opened up. And Parliament itself noted that the extension to Victoria had been suggested by a Royal Commission and abandoning it went against the spirit of things. Altogether it was not surprising that the Bill was thrown out on 14 May 1909.

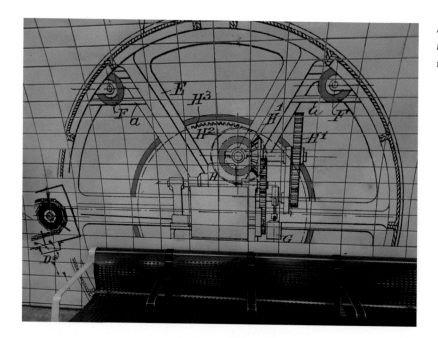

Modern platform decoration at Paddington, showing a design of tunnelling machine.

For the next two years the GWR and the Bakerloo sat there trying to bluff each other into making an offer. The Bakerloo hoped that the GWR would eventually see that a direct link to the West End was essential and so worth paying for. The GWR behemoth expected this upstart pipsqueak to see that it needed the traffic, claiming that it would provide 5 or 6 million new passengers each year. Who would blink first?

As it turned out, the Bakerloo did, for reasons we will see shortly. Their 1911 Bill (which received Royal Assent on 2 June that year) proposed a 972yd (889m) line that curved south under various properties and the east end of the Paddington canal basin before swinging round through about 120 degrees, skimming along Norfolk Mews (now Praed and London Mews), and then taking a 5-chain (100m) radius curve to once again end up under London Street by the station entrance, but, this time, facing north-west into its natural territories. The GWR were persuaded to contribute some money, but a mere £18,000 in instalments over eight years. The only significant objections were from the Metropolitan again, this time claiming that the GWR's payment breached an agreement from forty-six years earlier.

The extension, and the station at Paddington, opened on 1 December 1913. Having put some money in, the GWR cooperated in making the line a success, modifying the subway to the Inner Circle station (then called 'Praed Street') to give direct access to the Bakerloo booking office. They also started issuing through seasons to LER stations. The LER reciprocated by selling tickets to GWR stations as far as Reading and by making special arrangements for late-night passengers: tickets were collected on Bakerloo trains as soon as they departed from Edgware Road so that GWR passengers could simply run for their train without having to delay at the barriers.

Paddington was the first Bakerloo station, and only the third on the entire Underground after Earl's Court and Liverpool Street, to be equipped with escalators. There were two Otis A type machines with a fixed staircase between them (they have since been replaced by Otis's HD-B type). These were at a slope of 1 in 7 (about 26½ degrees), rather than the 30 degrees that is now normal on the Underground. More significantly, they were of the 'shunt' type: at the end of the escalator the side wall formed a diagonal across the treads, forcing the user to step off to one side while the treads disappeared under the resulting barrier. (Up escalators had a straight start, but down escalators were reversible and so had a diagonal shunt at both ends.) Unlike lift shafts at earlier stations, the escalators reached right down to platform level, meaning that the platform tunnels were further apart. (Otis Type As were also used at the Oxford Circus and Baker Street installations described earlier.)

But Paddington was no longer a destination, only a stopping point. Where was next?

Watford

Back in 1837, the London and Birmingham Railway (L&B) started a service from their station in Euston to Boxmoor, a town about 40km (24 miles) away to the north-west and just on the London side of the Chiltern Hills. The next year they completed the line all the way to Birmingham. In 1846, the GWR promoted a new line from Oxford to Birmingham, one which would give them their own route to the latter. In response, the London and Birmingham arranged a merger with the Manchester and Birmingham Railway and the Grand Junction Railway, which ran lines from Birmingham to Liverpool and Preston. The new company was called the LNWR and was to become the 'Premier Line', running trains along the length of England and, through cooperation with other companies to form the West Coast Main Line, all the way to Aberdeen. It was the largest joint stock company in the UK and certainly the largest railway company, though not necessarily the most profitable.

Despite their huge long-distance business, the L&B and then the LNWR had little interest in local traffic and probably contributed less to the growth of London than any of the other railways that served the metropolis. The original line to Boxmoor had only two intermediate stations, at Harrow (though on the low ground of the Weald rather than in the town itself) and at the market town of Watford. Even by 1900 there were only seven stations in the 28km (17½ miles) between the latter and Euston. More significantly, the company was only interested in long-distance traffic; they had good connections to

LNWR logo on Hatch End station.

the London docks in the east and to the lines south of the Thames, but these were primarily goods routes. Despite the complex set of junctions and huge yards still to be seen around Willesden, the station there was a mean and confusing place. As a result of this policy, these intermediate stations got only a sparse service compared with other lines. In 1879, there was only an hourly service to Watford and potential travellers at other stations might find they had a two- or three-hour wait for the next stopping train while expresses thundered through.

In the later part of the nineteenth century the company opened two short branches in the London area. The first, in 1862, was from Watford to the nearby town of Rickmansworth, while the second, in 1890, was from Harrow to the rural village of Stanmore. Both branches faced north from the main line, meaning that through trains (not that there were any) would have had to reverse at the junction station. Though run by the LNWR, both these lines had been promoted and built by outsiders – Baron Ebury, formerly the local MP, in the first case and a hotelier in the second. Both will appear again in our story. There was also a third branch from Watford to the city of St Albans, opened in 1858, but this was the first railway to that city and not intended as a commuter line.

At the start of the twentieth century the LNWR suddenly woke up to the dangers of their policy when, in 1901, a tube line was authorized from Golders Green all the way to Watford. The Metropolitan had a line running through Wembley, Harrow and Rickmansworth, all places that the LNWR had complacently thought were their own. Houses were starting to spring up in this area, but not around the LNWR's route. Something clearly needed to be done. So in 1906 they announced that they would be building a new suburban *electrified* railway line from Euston to Watford, mostly running alongside the existing route, with no less than sixteen intermediate stations.

For the most part, building this line would merely be expensive (£2,195,824, to be exact, excluding the power station and new trains); expensive because

the formation would have to be widened from four tracks to six, but 'merely' since the area was largely undeveloped, so there were no major obstacles in the way. The Willesden and Watford areas would be a bit harder, but nothing particularly unusual. It was the Euston end that would be the problem. The line out of Euston wanted to go west to reach Willesden, but Regent's Park and the built-up area of Lisson Grove were in the way. Instead, it had to head almost north, but was again blocked, this time by a ridge and the peak of Primrose Hill. As a result, the line climbs steeply to Camden at 1 in 77 (1.3 per cent) and then makes a sharp turn into the Primrose Hill tunnels. The original tunnel was 1,170yd (1,070m) long; when the line was quadrupled to Watford the two pairs of tracks were 'gauntleted' through it (interlaced to avoid the need for points at each end). Eventually a second tunnel opened in 1879 to the south of the first one, 12yd (11m) longer at the east end.

The new line needed to avoid congesting these tunnels. Therefore the LNWR went the whole hog and decided put the entire line in tunnel from east of Queen's Park all the way to Euston, where it would run in a big loop with a platform under the east side of the station, convenient for a subway to the Hampstead tube. Many commuters would therefore completely miss the main-line station. The tunnels would be 13ft 6in (4.1m) in diameter, too big for tube trains but too small for the normal main-line ones, meaning that the line would require dedicated

Southbound Bakerloo train on the New Lines near Kenton in 1928.
LCGB/LURS COLLECTION 06811

rolling stock, but, since this would be the LNWR's first electric service in the London area, that was not a major issue.

The whole 'New Lines' project (as it is still referred to today, though 'DC Lines' is also seen) was costed at £3.6 million and the relevant Act received Royal Assent on 26 July 1907. However, the money markets were about to go into depression again and the company had to shelve the project for a while.

We must now step back briefly to 1846, when the L&B promoted a company with the snappy title of the East and West India Docks and Birmingham Junction Railway and provided two-thirds of its funding. This 'independent' line (H.P. White described it in 1963 as having 'precisely the degree of freedom now ascribed to the satellites of Eastern Europe', referring to the days of the Soviet Union) was essentially a 13km (8-mile) branch from the east end of the Primrose Hill tunnels via Islington and Hackney to the docks at Poplar. In 1853, it was given the more manageable name of the North London Railway (NLR). Though it was primarily a goods line and initially ran through open countryside once out of the docks, it also built up a reasonable passenger traffic (over 4 million in 1853). In 1860, a 5½-mile (8.8km) connection was built from Camden to Willesden Junction via Hampstead and Brondesbury; through services then ran over the North and South Western Junction Railway (N&SWJR) to Kew and Richmond.

However, the NLR's connection to the City was very roundabout, with trains running all the way east to Bow before heading back to Fenchurch Street on the London and Blackwall Railway's tracks. So in 1865 the NLR opened a new branch south from Dalston to a terminus at Broad Street, next to – though much higher than – Liverpool Street station. Even though it was enormously expensive because it required building a wide viaduct through a built-up area, it quickly became known as the 'happy afterthought' for the effects it had on passenger numbers, which doubled in the first year. (Broad Street station has disappeared under the Broadgate

development, but most of the viaduct now carries the East London Line.)

In 1909, the LNWR gave up the pretence and took day to day control of the NLR – and also the N&SWJR – even though the companies remained legally separate until Grouping in 1922. They took the opportunity to rethink the New Lines plan to both improve it (after all, most passengers would not have Euston as their final destination) and reduce the costs. Under the new plan, services from Watford would be split into three separate streams. Some trains would still run to Euston, with two new single-track tunnels through Primrose Hill connecting to the existing surface tracks into the terminus, while others would turn left after those tunnels to run along the NLR lines to Broad Street. But it is the third stream that is the key part of our story: the Bakerloo Line would be extended from Edgware Road through Paddington and then come to the surface at Queen's Park station on the LNWR, meaning that Bakerloo trains could run all the way from Watford Junction to Elephant & Castle and give commuters a direct service into the West End.

The Extension Opens

The Bakerloo leapt at this proposal. It would more than quadruple the length of the line without costing anywhere near as much as that to build. It solved the question of which direction the Paddington station would face. And, best of all from their view, the LNWR was offering to lend them £1,000,000 at a mere 4 per cent interest and no time limit on repayment to help meet the costs of the works. Parliament approved the idea in 1912 and work started immediately. Despite the outbreak of World War I, the line was opened on 31 January 1915, though initially trains ran empty between Kilburn Park and Queen's Park while some final works were done on the latter; the full service opened eleven days later. Maida Vale was delayed by another four months or so by fitting-out problems, opening on 6 June. When it did open, it was the first station in London where everyone working there was female (though this claim has to be tempered by the fact that there

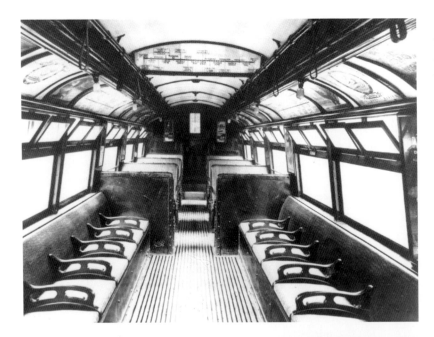

The interior of an early Bakerloo train; the seating layout suggests it's one of the original 1906 motor cars, though this picture was clearly taken after Queen's Park opened in 1915.
LURS COLLECTION CDWF02

A train of 1938 Stock comes out of Queen's Park north shed in 1985.
MALC MCDONALD

was a single male stationmaster for this station and three others). The initial service was 24tph in the peaks and 17tph at other times, taking 25 minutes for the full length of the journey.

The New Lines themselves had been opened from a temporary junction north of Kensal Green called 'Willesden Tunnel Mouth Junction' as far as Harrow in 1912, though the lines were not elec-trified and so steam trains were used instead. The rest of the line to Watford opened the following year. Meanwhile, construction continued south-wards from Willesden Tunnel Mouth, with two new tunnels 320yd (293m) long through the ridge just north of Kensal Green station. On 10 May 1915, everything was ready and the Bakerloo trains started running through to Willesden Junction. The initial service was a clockface one, with trains every quarter of an hour from about 05:30 to midnight on weekdays and every half hour from about 08:00 to 23:00 on Sundays. A few southbound trains in the morning did not stop at Queen's Park, Kilburn Park, or Warwick Avenue. Kensal Green station did not open until 1 October 1916.

The war delayed the rest of the construction work and so it was 16 April 1917 when the Bakerloo could finally run the rest of the way to Watford Junction, though initially only on weekdays (Sunday services started in July 1919). More wartime delays and shortages meant that it was 1922 before the new tunnels through Primrose Hill, at 1,452yd (1,328m) northbound and 1,264yd (1,156m) southbound, were ready. At the south end of these were complex junctions giving non-conflicting access to both Euston and the North London line. Meantime, electric trains started running on the line from Richmond and Kew to Broad Street in 1916.

The Route

Starting at Paddington station and climbing at an average of 1 in 200 (0.5 per cent), the line takes a gentle S-shaped curve under the higher-numbered platforms, the canal and a few wharfside buildings to run under Harrow Road (now Venice Walk) and the first stretch of Warwick Avenue (shown as Warwick Road on some contemporary maps). This is where the corresponding station is found, at the point where the road widens before the intersection with Clifton Villas (nowadays the road is split into two by parking areas). There is no surface building; the booking office is under the road and access is by staircases on each side of the road, occupying 'build-outs' that cars need to swing around. Unusually, both staircases have a glass screen over the top.

The line continues under Warrington Crescent before turning the corner into Randolph Avenue, passing under six or so properties in doing so. Maida Vale station lies immediately south-east of the intersection with Elgin Avenue, where the road is narrow enough that the platform tunnels encroach on the properties to either side. The booking office is still underground, but reached through a familiar-looking building on the corner. When Randolph Avenue, and then Gardens, run out, the line curves west to run across the street pattern (initially under St Augustine's schools, though at the time of construction it was under houses between the two schools, which have expanded towards each other) to Kilburn Park station at the intersection of Cambridge Avenue and Alpha Place. This time, the station building is large enough to have a booking office at ground level. All three of these stations are clearly built and decorated in the Leslie Green style, down to the oxblood tiles at the two surface stations, but postdate him by several years and

Kilburn Park station in earlier days.
LURS COLLECTION CDWF06

Kilburn Park station on a sunny day in June 2019. From the outside, little about the station has changed since it first opened, though the shop is new.

were almost certainly designed by his assistant and successor Stanley A. Heaps. All three had no lifts, but had a pair of Otis type A escalators with a staircase between; these have now been replaced with HD-Bs.

The tunnels continue under what was a row of narrow houses on Canterbury Road, but is now a block of 120 or so flats called Gorefield House. At this point it originally crossed on to LNWR territory where four pairs of sidings fed commercial properties on the other side of the road, but the area is now occupied by St Mary's RC primary school. Crossing the four main tracks and now climbing at 1 in 48 (2.1 per cent), it emerges between the two tracks of the New Lines next to a narrow carriage shed so as to enter Queen's Park station from the east end. Queen's Park was rebuilt as two island platforms, one for each direction, under an overall glass roof – the Bakerloo tracks are in the middle, with the New Lines on the outside. To the south are the four main-line tracks; the two nearest the

station still have their original platforms, though unused. Immediately west of the station is a four-car shed with the New Lines running either side of it. The central two tracks of this shed are sidings and originally had inspection pits, but the outer two are the running lines, merging into the New Lines tracks at the west end. This means that, uniquely, passengers ride through the shed in normal service, though the tracks can be used to store trains overnight.

The LNWR line is in a cutting from here to Willesden Junction, punctuated only by the tunnels west of Kensal Green station. While the four main-line tracks go through two traditional arch-shaped brick tunnels, the New Lines have two iron tubes driven by shields as if this were another tube line, though they are large enough to take a full-sized train. At Willesden Junction the line curves slightly to the right to go round what is now a small depot – but was a carriage shed – before entering the New Lines station. This is a thin oval with the through tracks curving around each side and a bay track down the middle to allow trains from London to reverse direction; it is still possible to walk from one side to the other at the west end of the station. Each side of the station has a roof over it. When first built, the main-line tracks also had platforms, but these have long gone. The NLR line splits into three pairs of tracks north-east of the station. One pair drops down to enter the station for the passenger service, while the second runs along the north side of the station, though at a higher level, before crossing over to meet the main tracks, allowing goods trains to avoid the curves of the station. Finally, the third pair crosses the entire LNWR line at right angles with platforms on the bridge and provides the route towards Richmond.

There are major yards on the west side of Willesden Junction station and the New Lines curve round them, calling at the new stations of Harlesden and Stonebridge Park on the way. The LNWR built a depot next to the latter to maintain its new electric trains. It then passes under the main tracks through the curiously named Intersection Tunnel (135yd [123m]) and turns back to line up with them at Wembley Central station. For the next 8km (5 miles) or so the New Lines run along the west side of the four main-line tracks. The three new stations on this section were designed by the LNWR to a common design that makes them look rather like a suburban bungalow stuck on or beside an overbridge. They contrast significantly with the Baroque revival Hatch End station designed by Gerald Horsley and built a few years earlier, or with the new buildings built on the north-east side of Harrow & Wealdstone station when it was expanded to accommodate the New Lines.

It is at Bushey that the project became more complicated. The main line runs along a high embankment between there and Watford Junction; widening it would have been a difficult task with various industrial buildings to move and under-line bridges to extend. The LNWR's disdain for suburban traffic also came back to bite it with a vengeance, because though there was some

Wall decoration at Maida Vale station; there is no ground floor, just stairs down to the booking hall.

housing to the north of the Junction station in the V between the main line and the St Albans branch, the town had developed mostly well to the west. Even the High Street was a good 800m (half a mile) walk along the Clarendon Road and the far end was perhaps twice as far. Fixing this would require major construction.

At Bushey, the New Lines run on a curved viaduct over the Colne Valley, turning more than 90 degrees to point west. The platforms at Bushey

Hatch End station, following the 1911 rebuild.

An example of the LNWR 'country bungalow' station style, this one at Headstone Lane.

A Bakerloo train shunts into the long 'Rickmansworth' platform at Watford Junction in 1962.

CQC/LURS COLLECTION 02146

station were not aligned with those on the existing tracks, but, rather, were on the start of the curve, their mid-points about 100m (330ft) further north. After crossing Dalton Way, the viaduct gives way to an embankment and, a short distance later, the location of Colne Junction. Here the New Lines originally split into two to form a triangular junction with the Rickmansworth branch: the left arm (now lifted) carried straight on to Croxley Junction, while the right one curves back again by 120 degrees to head towards Watford and meet the branch at Watford High Street Junction. The Rickmansworth branch already had a station where it ran under the lower end of the High Street, but since the line was single track the whole thing needed rebuilding. The island platform now lies within a brick-walled cutting and is covered with a peaked glass roof that is partially supported by ornamental trusses springing from the walls. At street level the simple building has a glass frontage that is nearly as big as itself. From here, the line curves back round to meet the main-line tracks as they enter Watford Junction, having taken more than 25 per cent longer – about 2,400m (2,600 yards) instead of 1,900m (2,100 yards), with an exact difference of 417m (1,368ft).

The entry of the New Lines resulted in significant expansion to this station. Originally there were

eight platforms, three (one a bay) for the St Albans branch, four for the through lines and one more for the Rickmansworth branch, though this last had connections at both ends so that it could also be used by trains on the down (northbound) fast track. To this were added three (later four) new bay platforms for the New Lines services. These consist of two 'peninsular' platforms with a crossbar at the northern end. This then had a wide wooden staircase down to the booking hall. The subway to the existing platforms was further north and did not serve the new ones (the new platforms are only about half the length of the older ones). The Rickmansworth branch closed to passengers in 1960 and soon afterwards its platform was cut back in line with the adjacent ones and dedicated to New Lines services. This also allowed a direct walking path to the northbound fast platform and its steps down to the subway, initially over a narrow and rather rickety footbridge.

One other piece of work was involved in the Watford area. A new single track branch line was taken off the Rickmansworth branch, immediately west of the triangular junction, heading to Cassio Bridge where the Watford to Rickmansworth road crosses the Grand Union Canal and the adjacent River Gade. The station sat on an embankment on the far side of the canal, high above the road

Croxley Green depot with four Oerlikons and one 1938 Stock train peeking out. LURS COLLECTION 01412

and far from significant habitation. Named after the Rickmansworth satellite of Croxley Green, it might possibly have attracted some of those living on its eastern side as being marginally closer than the Metropolitan station in the town. An intermediate station called Watford West was built about halfway along the branch and marked the south-west corner of the built-up area at the time of construction. The branch opened in 1912, was electrified in 1922 and closed officially in 2003, though trains had stopped running in 1996 when the bridge approaching the terminus was removed to allow the road underneath to be widened. For the last few years leading up to this the only service was a single return train in the very early morning; this was replaced by a taxi until the official closure. The importance of this branch to our story is the depot built next to Croxley Junction, where Bakerloo Line trains stabled overnight for many years (the entrance faced west, so arriving trains had to run past the junction along a siding beside the Rickmansworth branch and then reverse into the depot). Until 1941, tube trains to and from the depot would only use the north (to/from Watford) side of the triangle, not the south side.

In 1914, an additional station was opened at Carpenders Park, in the open countryside, to serve a nearby golf course. The timing was unfortunate: World War I started soon afterwards and at the start of 1917 a general 'restraint on travel' was introduced by the government, meaning that the station closed again a few months before the Bakerloo

POLITICAL ACTION

On the evening of Sunday 9 March 1913, a group of young ladies stopped Police Constable Hagger walking his beat in Croxley Green and asked the way to the station. At around 01:45 the following morning, an incendiary device started a fire that destroyed the station building and the wooden platform. On Tuesday morning the stationmaster received a suffragette newspaper with 'Afraid copy left got burnt' written on the wrapping. The line only appears to have been closed for a day or so, suggesting a temporary platform was quickly constructed, though full rebuilding was delayed until the following year.

Croxley Green station after the suffragette attack. JOHN MANN

Less than an hour earlier on the same night the station at Saunderton, about 28km (17 miles) away, was destroyed by an explosion and multiple fires. A car-full of women was seen in the area.

service could reach it, not to reopen until 1919. Only nine days after this closure another one occurred when Stonebridge Park station caught fire, reopening at the start of August.

The original Carpenders Park station after housing had reached it. H.C. CASSERLEY

The LNWR built a new power station for the line close to Stonebridge Park station. This opened for service in 1916; until then, the LNWR ran steam trains and the Bakerloo trains to Willesden Junction were powered from the Underground system. Substations were installed at Queen's Park, Willesden Junction, Stonebridge Park, Kenton, Headstone Lane and Bushey, as well as at various places on the Richmond to Broad Street and (later) the Euston to Queen's Park sections.

Once fully open, the new route to Watford was a success. The initial service consisted of 4tph, though with no trains on Sundays, presumably extending the previous Willesden Junction service. The end to end time was sixty-three minutes, though this was aided by not stopping at Maida Vale and Regent's Park (in the peaks the Watford service also omitted Headstone Lane, Kenton and North Wembley, leaving those to the LNWR, plus Queen's Park and Kilburn Park). At last, the inhabitants of the area had a direct route to the West End

and south London. There were technical advantages too: connecting the Bakerloo to the rest of the rail network meant that trains could be moved to other lines by rail rather than one car at a time on a road trailer being pulled by one or even two traction engines. This was particularly useful for stock exchanges with the Piccadilly, which could be done via the District Line and its connections to Willesden Junction.

On the other hand, the mixture of main-line sized trains and the small tube trains meant that station platforms on the shared section were at the wrong height for at least one, if not both. The solution adopted was the use of a compromise height, meaning that passengers stepped up more than usual into main-line trains, but down into Bakerloo trains. Another problem was that the trains were, for the first time, running in the open. This introduced a new risk of disruption: snow, frost or frozen sleet forming an insulating layer on the current rails. The initial solution was to add wire brushes to

Sleet brushes.

the shoebeams carrying the current pick-up shoes, which would break up ice and push off snow. The LNWR also added brushes to some vans, which were then pushed along the line by steam locomotives.

The one party that was not happy with this was, of course, the Metropolitan. On learning of the LNWR proposals, they applied for Parliamentary powers to build a branch line to Watford. These were granted in 1912, though it was to be the end of 1925 before the branch opened.

WATFORD STADIUM

In 1976, the pop singer Elton John bought Watford Football Club and became its chairman. With his money poured into the club, by 1982 it had climbed from the bottom to the top of the football league. In an attempt to keep the much bigger 'away' crowds from the Junction station (this being the heyday of football hooliganism), a station was opened close to the club's Vicarage Road stadium, with the obvious name of Watford Stadium. Only open on match days, it suffered as the club's period of success ended. The last recorded train ran in 1993.

CHAPTER 7

Improvements

World War I

Back on the original Bakerloo route, World War I had various effects, most down to the threat of air raids. During the war London was bombed between twenty and thirty times (sources disagree) by airships and aircraft. These were small numbers by World War II standards, but the novel exposure to attack greatly disturbed the populace. The airships (mostly, though not all, Zeppelins) were particularly feared because they could approach silently, only starting their engines to escape after dropping their bombs; they were known as 'baby killers' to the British.

One concern was the possibility of a bomb hitting the underwater section of the Bakerloo. The first defence was a set of four crude floodgates fitted at the south end of Embankment station and the north end of Waterloo. Each consisted of a steel frame into which timber baulks could be dropped; the process took the best part of an hour to do and probably longer to undo. Engineers came up with plans for electrically moved floodgates, but the authorities refused to provide steel or any workable alternative for the purpose. Eventually a different approach was taken: the Bakerloo tunnels were lined with armour plate where they ran under the river (more precisely, for 480ft (145m) of the northbound tunnel and 540ft (165m) of the southbound).

For most of the circumference of the tunnel the plate was mounted immediately inside the rim, but under the track it consisted of a flat plate with the segment underneath filled with concrete. Special rails were used to reduce the height of the track, mounted on longitudinal timbers rather than the usual sleepers. The area outside the timbers was also filled with concrete.

As soon as it became clear that bombing was a real threat, plans were made to allow those caught in the street to shelter at tube stations without needing to pay for a ticket and eventually eighty-six stations were made available for this purpose. However, a spate of raids in September 1917 caused over 100,000 people to rush to the tubes even before the alarms were sounded and even on nights when there were no raids. On 28 September the rules were changed to forbid such access until there was an actual warning. However, this did not stop people and it is estimated that at the peak 300,000 people were sheltering in tube stations. To add insult to injury, some would ride the trains for free to alleviate boredom.

More generally, the war caused serious over-crowding as rail travel became more popular, increasing by 67 per cent over the four years. In late 1917, the Bakerloo service consisted of 24tph peak and 16tph off-peak to Queen's Park, with a further 4tph to Watford. No new stock was available, preventing trains from being lengthened. One attempt to control crowds that was tried in May 1917 at Oxford Circus was to place barriers along part of the length of the platform with sliding bars that were only opened after passengers had had a chance to alight. This was extended to Embankment in November and Piccadilly Circus the following spring. In September 1918, they were replaced by a system of queues at each boarding point, which remained in use until the end of the following year. Neither approach actually gained much because drivers needed more time to stop their trains in exactly the right place, while they required more than fifty extra staff to implement.

There was a 30 per cent fare increase in 1917, which, combined with the increased usage, meant that the LER was able to pay a 2 per cent dividend, enough to keep the shareholders from revolting, but not enough to make new tube railways a good investment. On 12 December 1916, Albert Stanley – Managing Director of the UERL – left to become an MP and President of the Board of Trade. He returned in 1919 and, for his service, became Baron Ashfield of Southwell in the 1920 New Year Honours List.

The Interwar Years

The twenty years between the wars were not ones of major change for the Bakerloo, but, rather, of incremental improvement. The period saw major social changes along the entire line. The presence of convenient transport made the West End – particularly Oxford Street and Regent Street – a major shopping and entertainment area instead of what it used to be: middle- and upper-class residences. Famous department stores like Dickens & Jones and Swan & Edgar were conveniently reached by the Bakerloo Line – the latter even gained its own subway to Piccadilly Circus station – and theatres and cinemas were clearly signed at nearby stations. The Bakerloo encouraged this traffic because it filled the otherwise largely empty off-peak trains.

In October 1919, Frank Pick (Stanley's deputy) proposed two new tube lines across London,

roughly at right angles, to relieve pressure on the existing ones and connect main lines on either side; this might be seen as an early forerunner of the Elizabeth Line. The north–south line would have duplicated much of the Bakerloo, branching off the Metropolitan in the St John's Wood area, then calling at Baker Street, Oxford Circus, Trafalgar Square, Waterloo and Elephant & Castle, before heading towards both Sevenoaks and Addington. However, there was no government support and the UERL could not afford such a large project without it.

This period could easily be called 'the decades of the escalator'. Escalators are far more convenient than lifts: there is no waiting around for the escalator to arrive and they can easily carry 10,000 passengers per hour. One escalator in each direction is therefore the equivalent of six fifty-person lifts of typical descent. Furthermore, if the escalator breaks down people can still walk up or down it. There is no waiting for the lift to be wound down by hand or another one to be brought alongside, nor are emergency staircases needed. Adding escalators from new, as on the extension to Queen's Park, is fairly easy, but replacing lifts with them has been described as an exercise in solid geometry; all too often the obvious route for the angled escalator shaft goes straight through the vertical lift shaft! The material above the London Clay is usually soft and soggy. It is one thing to push a metal cylinder vertically through it, but very much another to dig through it at an angle, though later on freezing techniques and chemical treatments to solidify the ground became available.

Waterloo gained two escalators in 1919 and a further three in 1928. In the latter case the wide shaft had to fit between two of the piers holding up the main-line railway; the clearance was only 2in (5cm) on each side. The area under the piers was carefully excavated and then filled with concrete – high strength under the piers, but much weaker where the tunnel would eventually be driven. Six other piers had to have 10ft (3m) wide passages cut through them to provide access between the escalators and the ticket hall.

Escalators at St John's Wood; the uplighters are part of the original design.

In 1926, the layout at Embankment was improved by tripling the size of the surface booking hall and adding two new escalators from the inter-mediate level to the new Hampstead line platform, coming into use in September. Later on escalators were also added from the booking hall to the inter-mediate level. In the same year Trafalgar Square gained two Otis type L escalators to replace its lifts. Although the early type Ls used the same shunt arrangement as the type As, in 1924 the present-day comb arrangement was introduced and the early installations converted.

There was yet another fare rise in 1920. What was special about this one is that the legal limit on tube fares was raised as a five-year experiment and it was now allowed to charge 1½d per mile or 2d for journeys under a mile. At the same time, Lord Ashfield tried to get rid of the 'dole to working men' of the workmen's fare, though he had to be satisfied with the end time being cut back to 07:30 from 08:00.

In 1921, Kilburn Park became the test bed for a new station arrangement called the 'passimeter'. A passimeter was a free-standing kiosk sitting at the barrier line, combining the role of ticket office and ticket inspection point. Passengers with a season or return ticket could just walk past it showing their ticket. Others would stop at one of the windows and buy a ticket, then enter the 'paid' part of the station. Usually there was a gate or barrier controlled from inside to just stop people walking past without paying. The passimeter became a popular feature of stations and many, if not most, had them for many years, though all have now gone.

This was also the year of the Grouping, when the Railways Act 1921 combined about one hundred and twenty railway companies into four large ones – the 'Big Four'. An early plan had seven compa-nies, one of which would have been 'railways in London', but the final one split the country roughly into sectors that met at the capital. This made it almost impossible to come up with the 'right' place for any of the Underground lines, so it was decided to leave them alone to be dealt with by a separate Act 'later'. Much later, as it turned out.

Passimeter, believed to be at Kilburn Park. LURS COLLECTION 86KA20

On 13 May 1924, an unusual event occurred on a Bakerloo Line train at Elephant & Castle: Mrs Daisy Hammond gave birth to a baby daughter. The story has grown up that the little girl was named Thelma Ursula Beatrice Eleanor, but this appears to have been a press fabrication and her actual name was Mary Ashfield Eleanor, though various sources name her instead as Marie Cordery. Lord Ashfield became her godfather, saying 'Of course it would not do to encourage this sort of thing as I am a busy man.' Since then, six other babies have been born on the Underground:

- Jennifer, born to Julia Kowalska at Kingsbury, 19 December 2008
- boy born to Michelle Jenkins at London Bridge, 28 May 2009
- Highbury & Islington, 21 February 2017
- boy at Warren Street, 15 January 2019
- girl at Westminster, 14 July 2019
- girl at Baker Street, 11 October 2019.

The Metropolitan Railway finally opened its branch into Watford, to compete with the LNWR (now the London Midland and Scottish Railway (LMSR)) and Bakerloo joint service, on 2 November 1925. They had originally aimed at an unused piece of land close to the north end of the High Street, nicely complementing the LMSR station at the south end, but this route would have run across Cassiobury Park and the local council objected. Instead, they were left with a station on the edge of the park and beside a new estate in west Watford, around 1,200m (¾ of a mile) from their objective. While the line gained some patronage from both this area and other new housing on the other side of the park, plus a bit more from a bus service to the town centre that the Metropolitan ran, it never met its original objective of providing effective competition.

Returning to central London, this period saw various major station rebuilds in the centre, two of which affected the Bakerloo. The first was Oxford Circus, which was now the second busiest station on the Underground. The pre-war improvements to join the two stations into one had helped, but were now insufficient. So the Bakerloo ticket hall was further extended under Argyll Street and now became the ticket hall for all passengers, while the Central Line surface station just became another entrance. Two more type Otis type L (comb) escalators were added in a new shaft down to just above the Central Line. These changes came into use in 1925. Over the next few years the two existing Bakerloo escalators were converted to type L after a

Piccadilly Circus booking hall; although refurbished, it is very much in the style of the original.

third one was added in a separate shaft. This would not be the last redesign of this station, though that story comes later.

The biggest piece of reconstruction, however, came at Piccadilly Circus. Unlike Oxford Circus, this had always been a single station serving two lines, but in its first fifteen years the number of passengers had grown from 1.5 million to 18 million and in the next five years that would become 25 million. The ticket hall could not be expanded further (more space had been added in 1917) and passengers had to wait for lifts down to their platform, or, rather, down to the start of a long walk to their platform. It was clear that the only option was to build a brand new station from scratch underneath Piccadilly Circus itself. The work would take 4 years, from 1924 to 1928, and cost £500,000, but it would produce a station capable of handling 50 million passengers a year.

The new booking hall is an ellipse 155 × 144ft (47.2 × 44m) under the roadway and pavement with four subways leading to seven separate stair-

case exits scattered around the road junction and to three shop basements. From the ellipse two banks of escalators, one of three and one of two, descend to a lower concourse from which a bank of three escalators serves each line; the Piccadilly then has two separate staircases down to cross-passages between the platforms, while the Bakerloo has two staircases to each platform. There are also two connecting passages between the lines. The various pipes and sewers in the area were diverted into a separate 550ft (170m) long subway. The booking hall is decorated in marble and bronze and there were originally oil paintings above the top of the escalators (now replaced by advertisements). When opened, there were twenty-eight ticket machines in banks of seven, selling pre-printed tickets at prices from 1d to 6d (including 1½d) – each machine had a list of destinations for the relevant price on it – though these have long since been replaced by a modern gateline.

The work was done without disturbing the road traffic. This meant sinking a shaft 18ft (5.5m) in diameter to provide access for the works. The only place available was the site of the statue and fountain generally known as 'Eros', though it is actually of the Greek god Anteros – the god of requited love – and is correctly known as the Shaftesbury Memorial Fountain. The new station was opened on 10 December 1928 by the Mayor of Westminster. The original Leslie Green station building was closed the next year and demolished in the 1980s. The station suffered from leaks after rain and remedial work had to be done in 1931 and 1932.

During the 1920s the local councils in the southeast of London were demanding a tube line even though there were dense networks of railways already, many in the process of electrification. It was in 1930 that a development scheme for the Elephant & Castle area was announced that would require destruction of the C&SLR station there and reconstruction of the Bakerloo station to handle all the traffic. The UERL announced that it could actually save money by extending the Bakerloo at the same time; doing so would reduce the number of passengers boarding and alighting at Elephant and so the extent of the works required. Therefore

it agreed to extend the line along the line of the Walworth Road and Camberwell Road (though not sticking exactly to them) to a depot at Denmark Hill and stations at Albany Road and Camberwell Green. Parliamentary powers were granted in 1931, but money dried up *again* and the only tunneling work done was to divert the sidings beyond Elephant & Castle station along the new route, destroying the old ones, and lengthening them to around the junction with Elephant Road; the new sidings are 157m (515ft) long. However, the remaining powers have never been abandoned.

Meanwhile, the Bakerloo service kept running. The typical peak service in the late 1920s was 26tph with six-car trains. In 1933, 4tph were extended from Queen's Park to Harrow & Wealdstone, giving the southern half of the New Lines an 8tph service of Bakerloo trains. One problem that had bedeviled passengers for many years was that, due to the lack of train indicators at stations and only one small sign on the front of the trains, they had no idea where a train would be terminating. So in June 1932 the cream upper panels of the trains were split by a thick blue horizontal line on those that ran beyond Queen's Park.

Elephant & Castle sidings south of the station.

In 1933 the Underground introduced another design classic: Harry Beck's diagrammatic map. Up to then it was normal for maps of the system to be largely geographic (though the Metropolitan had a tendency to 'adjust' the scale north of Harrow), meaning that stations were crowded together in the middle and spread out at the edges. It was common for a line to end, not at a terminus, but at a box listing half a dozen stations that wouldn't fit on the map. Beck abandoned this approach and introduced the one we are so familiar with, based on electrical circuit diagrams. Stations are evenly spaced, lines are horizontal, vertical, or on 45-degree diagonals, and there is no attempt to match geography, just relationships. The map is so popular that most travellers have little or no idea what the geography of the Underground is actually like.

Meanwhile, government had been, at its usual breakneck speed, considering the question of what to do with the railways in London after leaving them out of Grouping. It was a knotty problem, as they couldn't even figure out who actually controlled the UERL, since the controlling votes were held by bearer bonds, which had no owner – if you held the piece of paper, you had the vote. The eventual government decision was that a new body would be created that owned all the railways in London other than those run by the 'Big Four' and would also be given a monopoly of road transport – buses, coaches, trams and later on trolleybuses – in the controlled area. This was far bigger than London; it stretched to Guildford, Sevenoaks, Harlow, Hemel Hempstead and Slough. The body would be run as a commercial enterprise and had shares (in five classes) that would be issued to the shareholders of the existing companies – notably the UERL – that would be merged into it and to the local councils who were giving up their bus companies and tramways. The seven members of the board would be appointed by a panel of neutral trustees, so that this would not be nationalization and government control. The Metropolitan, naturally, fought this proposal tooth and nail. Having denied that it was a main-line railway in order to escape Grouping, it now insisted it *was* one to avoid being absorbed. But this time it lost the fight.

And so, on 1 July 1933, the London Passenger Transport Board (LPTB) came into existence. Lord Ashfield was its chairman and Frank Pick his deputy; the other members were a union representative, a director of the Bank of England, two local politicians and a highway engineer. The prospective LPTB had also reached agreement with the main-line railways to pool all receipts in the controlled area: the LPTB received 62 per cent; the Southern Railway 25.5 per cent; and the other three the remaining 12.5 per cent (the exact proportions were agreed to the precision of £1 in £10 million). This meant that there was no longer a need to compete for traffic.

Two days after the LPTB took over, the Bakerloo gained a new station – the last on its present route – at South Kenton. However, this can hardly be counted toward the board's credit. The first action visible to Bakerloo passengers was that, in late May 1934, the 'UNDERGROUND' on the side of trains was replaced by 'London Transport – Bakerloo Line'.

An Act of 1936 gave the LPTB the power to extend all Bakerloo station platforms (except at Baker Street, which had already been done) to hold eight-car trains. In practice, they were extended from 291ft (89m) to 377ft (115m), allowing seven-car trains. This explains why some platforms are curved at one end: the original platform was straight, but the line had a curve immediately afterwards.

Despite the reorganization, the LPTB still struggled with money. Four of the five classes of London Transport shares had fixed dividend rates, leaving only the 'C' stock with any flexibility. This was supposed to receive 5.5 per cent but never did; the best year was 4.25 per cent and the average over the first five years was just under 4 per cent. The shortfall in that best year represented a mere one-fiftieth of a penny per passenger, yet the gap was never closed. By 1940, the Board would need an increase in income of £3 million to keep up.

Through the 1920s and 1930s a tide of suburban housing flooded out over the area that had been countryside, mostly from the nuclei of railway stations rather than through growth of existing towns, to form what we know as Greater London. The Bakerloo and its major rival the Metropolitan drove this growth in the north-west. Though they only met directly once after leaving Baker Street – a bridge in the suburb of Kenton where the Metropolitan crosses over the West Coast Main Line and thus the Bakerloo – they fought for custom in Wembley, Harrow and Watford.

But something was about to happen to the rivals.

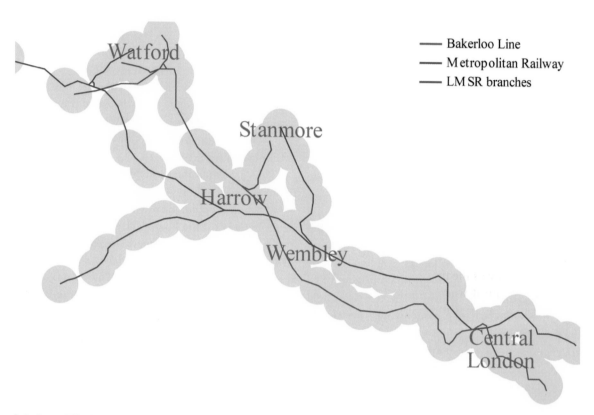

—— Bakerloo Line
—— Metropolitan Railway
—— LMSR branches

Bakerloo and Metropolitan lines in 1935 showing the conflicts. Each circle has a radius of 1 km (⅝ mile), about 10 to 15 minutes' walk.

CHAPTER 8

Stanmore

The Metropolitan Railway

The Metropolitan Railway has appeared many times already in these pages, but it is time to look at it in more detail. When the railway opened its 5.91km (3.68 miles) line under the Euston Road in 1863, it was the first underground railway in the world. But it was not to stay that way for long. Within five years it had constructed a short branch that was to make it schizophrenic for well over a century, ending only in 1990 with a full split.

One half of the Metropolitan is the 'City' section, now renamed the Hammersmith & City Line. Though using full-sized trains, it is no different in principle to the Bakerloo, connecting places in central London and the inner suburbs. It quickly threw out branches to Hammersmith and Kensington (the latter now closed) and curved round at both ends to meet its child and rival, the Metropolitan District, to form the Inner Circle.

The other half is variously 'the Extension' and 'the Main Line'. This started life in 1868 as a 2.84km (1¾-mile) branch from Baker Street to Swiss

Metropolitan Railway electric loco 7 Edmund Burke pulls a fast train towards West Hampstead before the arrival of the Bakerloo.
LOCOMOTIVE & GENERAL

Cottage, but, like Topsy, it 'growed'. Even in 1885, a government inspector was to say that it 'practically speaking, is not a Metropolitan Railway'. By 1892, it had reached the neighbourhood of what would become Milton Keynes and by 1899 it was a mere 16km (10 miles) from Oxford and was carrying express trains from Manchester. It is this half we are interested in.

The detailed reasons for this growth are mostly outwith the scope of this book, but two specific causes can be noted. First, in its early years the Metropolitan came under the control of one of the great railway empire builders, Edward Watkin, who ran railways all over the world. In particular, Watkin pushed the Metropolitan to cooperate with the Manchester, Sheffield and Lincolnshire Railway (which became the Great Central Railway), resulting in the latter reaching London over Metropolitan rails. He also tried to link these with the South Eastern Railway with the intent of creating a route from Manchester to Paris via a Channel Tunnel. Second, the Metropolitan had an unusual legal position. When most railways bought land during construction and didn't use it, they had to dispose of it again. The Metropolitan, on the other hand, was allowed to keep that land and develop it for housing. This gave it an inbuilt incentive to build

lines to green-field sites and then make money out of urbanizing them, resulting in the phenomenon known as 'Metro-land'. (The term was first used in publicity material in May 1915; the presence or absence of a hyphen varied over the years.)

At the start of 1932 the trunk of the Metropolitan ran 81.08km (about 50½ miles) from Baker Street to the hamlet of Verney Junction in Buckinghamshire, with four branches: 11.25km (7 miles) to Uxbridge; 3.31km (just over 2 miles) to Watford; 6.35km (just under 4 miles) to Chesham; and 10.6km (6.6 miles) to Brill on the Oxfordshire/Buckinghamshire border. All except the first 3.39km (2.1 miles) was on the surface, not in tunnel. The line was six-tracked from Finchley Road, where it came to the surface, to Harrow-on-the-Hill (two of these were dedicated to Great Central Railway – now the London and North Eastern Railway (LNER) – traffic to Marylebone, while the other four were for the Metropolitan itself) and electrified as far north as Rickmansworth.

On 10 December 1932, with the LPTB already on the horizon, the Metropolitan opened its fifth and last branch, from Wembley Park to the small rural village of Stanmore. Stanmore already had one railway line. In 1882, the hotel magnate Frederick Gordon had acquired the mansion of Bentley

Stanmore station under construction.
R.J. GREENAWAY/LURS COLLECTION 04480

Priory and turned it into a country hotel for the wealthy. To make it more attractive, he promoted and, in 1890, opened a railway from the edge of Stanmore to Harrow & Wealdstone on the LNWR. The Metropolitan's new line, however, was a naked attempt to promote the urbanization of the area between Wembley and Edgware and capture some of the traffic currently going to the LER's station at the latter. Initially the branch had 3tph to Wembley Park, plus 3tph through to Baker Street. The trains tended to be rather empty, since in the first couple of years there was little or no new development around the three intermediate stations and it probably did not help that the fares were much higher than the LER's. For example, the 7d fare for a direct journey from Edgware to Embankment was less than half the 1s. 3d fare from Stanmore with one or even two changes of train on the way.

Whether they carried passengers or not, the Stanmore branch trains were adding to the Metropolitan's congestion problem. The line was seeing around 24tph in the peak hours, which might not seem much until one looked at the details of the layout. The four-track section (ignoring the tracks to Marylebone) consisted of separate fast and slow pairs that exchanged sides at Wembley Park, causing a conflict for every train running north of there, then at Finchley Road the two pairs combined into one, meaning that the northbound fast trains crossed the path of the southbound slows. The latter was worsened by the fact that a large number of extra trains started south of Wembley Park. Finally, there were three stops for slow trains on the section between Finchley Road and Baker Street.

Clearly something had to be done to relieve this bottleneck, but what? The original line had been cut-and-cover and there was absolutely no way permission was going to be given to dig up Finchley Road or – even worse – Lord's Cricket Ground again. In 1925, the Metropolitan had looked at building a new tube line 4.97km (3.09 miles) long; this would start west of Kilburn station, diving down from the embankment the existing line occupied to run deep under the Edgware Road to the Paddington area, where it would swing round to rise and enter the Metropolitan's Edgware Road station at the western end. This would require a tube big enough to take the full-sized trains that the Metropolitan used, greatly increasing the cost of the project (estimated at just over £2 million), and would result in three routes converging at two flat junctions just west of the station. Various things caused a delay until 1928, at which point the Ministry of Transport published new rules requiring all trains in tube tunnels to have carriages arranged so that in an emergency passengers could leave at either end of the train. This would have required rebuilding all the Metropolitan's express stock and they abandoned the plan. In the end, the only work that was done was to rebuild Edgware Road station with two island platforms and make provision in the resulting resignalling for the two sets of points and six extra signals that would be required. One effect of this was that the train indicators added as part of the work – and now long gone – had provision for destinations that could not be reached, such as Amersham and even Verney Junction.

A second plan was floated in 1930, involving a new main-line-sized tube running under the existing lines to Baker Street and then ascending to join the Circle. This was then reduced to a much simpler arrangement, whereby a short tube from Swiss Cottage and then a flyover would carry the northbound fast line out of the way of the southbound slow; this would address one conflict but not the congestion. But neither of these saw the light of day.

The arrival of the LPTB in 1933 provided a wider canvas for the planners to work on. The Metropolitan needed extra capacity, while the Bakerloo had spare capacity. Why not join the two together? Now that commercial rivalries weren't in the way and the government was willing to provide cheap credit for public works projects that would stimulate employment, it was an obvious solution to the problem. Because tube trains would be using the new tunnels, they could be smaller, bringing the costs down. On the other hand, tube trains were not really designed for long journeys, so it needed to be the short-distance trains that went through the new tunnels. That meant major rearrangements on

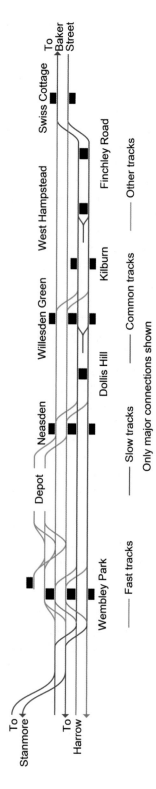

The Metropolitan main-line layout before the 1939 changes, showing the bottlenecks at Wembley Park and Finchley Road.

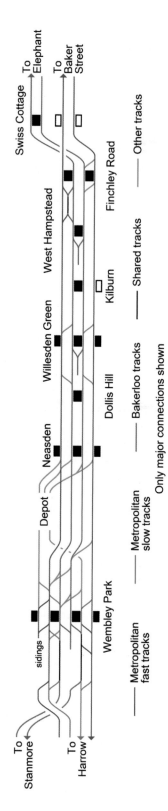

The Metropolitan main-line layout after the 1939 changes with the Bakerloo added.

the surface, though these were still cheaper than large tunnels. The Bakerloo was to take over the Stanmore branch and replace the services starting from Wembley Park, Neasden and Willesden Green; from now on Metropolitan trains would only stop at Wembley Park and Finchley Road. For the same reasons, the three stations in the existing tunnel would be closed, replaced by two in the new ones. It was blithely assumed that, with improved signalling and a third platform at Elephant & Castle (never built), the line could handle 23tph from the Queen's Park direction and 17tph from Stanmore.

To eliminate the various conflicts, the four-track section would be completely rearranged, with the Metropolitan tracks on the outside and the Bakerloo ones in the middle, while the flat junction on the slow tracks north of Wembley Park would be replaced by a new diveunder. The changes needed to achieve this would be complex and involve moving two stations (West Hampstead and Dollis Hill) sideways, adding a new island platform at Finchley Road, and completely replacing the signalling with six new signal boxes controlling 538 new signals. The rearrangement was done in two stages. On the weekend of 17/18 September 1938, the lines changed between Finchley Road and north of Dollis Hill, with a temporary junction to bring trains back to their old lines, then on the weekend of 5/6 November the rest of the line was rearranged. Compared with modern timescales this work was done incredibly fast. In both cases the work couldn't start until after the Saturday lunchtime rush hour (between the wars people normally worked 5½ days a week), two tracks had to reverse direction, old signals had to be removed and new ones commissioned and tested, yet even so a limited service was run on the new layout on the Sunday afternoon. The Bakerloo finally started running through the new tunnels and over these lines to Stanmore on 20 November 1939.

The Route and Stations

The new branch leaves the original Bakerloo at Baker Street station. A new southbound platform was added on the same level as and converging with the existing southbound, with cross-passages between them; the lines join at a junction under Cornwall Terrace. The majority of the junction was built around the existing tunnel with trains running through, though the narrowest part had to be done outside traffic hours, and until relatively recently the trailing points were spring-loaded rather than being worked by a signalman. Two new escalators were added from these cross-passages to the same circulating area as the 1914 ones. A single northbound platform was retained, with the new tunnel branching off where the line crosses Glentworth Street. This layout provided operational convenience – trains from one branch could be held in a platform to let one from the other branch depart – but was awkward for passengers: in the southbound direction there were two platforms with trains to the same destinations to choose from, while in the northbound direction passengers for the two branches had to mingle on the same platform and hope that the train indicators were correct. In fact, these were late in being fitted and in the meantime trains for the new branch carried a large diamond bearing the letter 'M' on the front.

The two tunnels then run west and curve round to the north. The southbound passes under Dorset Square and Marylebone station, while the northbound clips the southern edge of both, though it manages to get underneath the convent on Harewood Avenue. After crossing the Grand Union Canal they meet the Metropolitan at the southern end of Wellington Road (also the south-east corner of Lord's). They run under the Metropolitan as far as Circus Road, then diverge slightly eastwards to St John's Wood station, which replaced both its namesake at Lord's and Marlborough Road just to the north at the corner of Queen's Road (now Queen's Grove). From here, they run northwards under St John's Wood Park, parallel to the Metropolitan under Finchley Road, then turn under Avenue Road to reach the Swiss Cottage road junction and the station of the same name, which replaced the corresponding Metropolitan station. They then resume running under Finchley Road and the Metropolitan

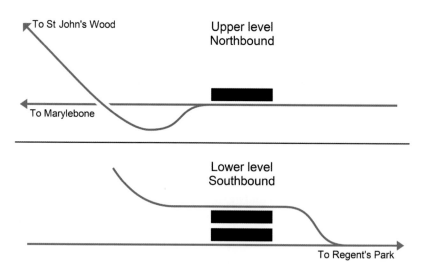

To St John's Wood

Upper level
Northbound

To Marylebone

Layout of Baker Street tube station from 1939 to 1979.

Lower level
Southbound

To Regent's Park

to Finchley Road station. The tunnel section was fitted from new with two approaches to reducing the noise level in the passenger compartments: welded rails and tunnel screens. The latter consists of a thin horizontal layer of concrete at about (train) floor level with a sound-absorbing layer on the under side.

The two new tube stations are very different on the outside, but very similar inside, having been both designed by Stanley Heaps. Neither bears any resemblance to the Leslie Green designs found on the original route. St John's Wood station is a rectangular building with a circular upper storey letting light into the booking hall. Beside the entrance are spaces for shops, while the space between the building and the road is occupied by small gardens and tall trees. Unfortunately, the whole effect is spoiled because somebody later allowed a seven-storey sixteen-sided white tower block, totally out of sympathy with the original design, to be built on top. Swiss Cottage, on the other hand, consists of a dark tower with an Underground logo at the top guarding a staircase down to the booking hall under the road, with passageways leading to three other entrances around the intersection. Each station has a pair of escalators, with a fixed stairway between, leading from the booking office down to platform level; the station tunnels are placed far enough apart to accommodate this. The lighting

is indirect, with the light from uplighters on small pillars reflecting off the ceiling of the shaft. At platform level the tiling is a light biscuit colour with panels marked out with a brown edge. For the first time on the Underground, the station name was repeated along the tiling just above eye level. More subtly, occasional tiles are not plain, but, rather, have moulded relief designs by the artist Harold Stabler; there are a total of eighteen different

Table 2   Harold Stabler's tiles

Description	Notes
Eagle	Bedfordshire
Five crowned maidens	Berkshire
Swan and crown	Buckinghamshire
Three scimitars	Essex
Stag and river	Hertfordshire
Rearing horse	Kent
Lion and river	County of London
Crown & three scimitars	Middlesex
Crowned oak leaf	Surrey
Five martlets	Westminster
Circle-and-bar	LPTB logo
Winged griffin	LPTB logo
55 Broadway	LPTB headquarters
Houses of Parliament	
St Paul's Cathedral	
Crystal Palace	
Five seagulls and river	River Thames
Bust of Thomas Lord	Lord's Cricket Ground

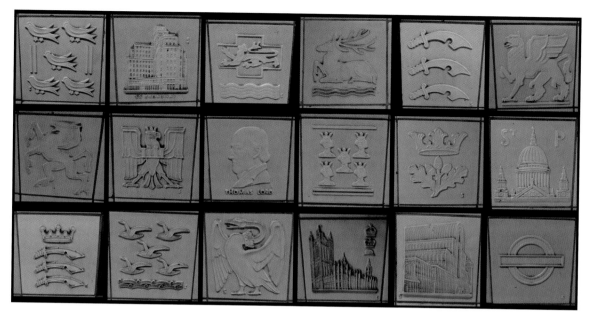

Stabler's tiles.

designs. These also originally appeared on the new platform at Baker Street and at St Paul's, but have been replaced, and some can still be seen at Aldgate East and Bethnal Green. The only significant difference between the two stations is that the secondary colour of some borders is yellow at St John's Wood and a jade green at Swiss Cottage.

Before the reconstruction, Finchley Road station – where the line emerges from tunnel – had an island platform on the slow lines (on the south side) with nothing on the fasts, the junction being in the mouth of the tunnel. A new tunnel needed to be excavated for the southbound fast line, running across the road and then under houses as far as opposite the end of Fairfax Road, then converging to meet the original about 100m (330ft) further east. This gave enough room for the new Bakerloo tunnels to climb up and pop out into the two central tracks. The tunnel started far enough north to allow a second island platform to be added. Both platforms are on a significant curve as the line leaves the route of the road and turns to head west towards Kilburn. Finchley Road became (and still is) a stop for all Metropolitan trains, allowing cross-platform interchange with the Bakerloo.

From here, the line runs roughly westwards to Wembley Park, mostly without major earthworks, though there is one long stretch of embankment and viaduct. There are six tracks throughout. From north to south they are – using the original nomenclature – the southbound Metropolitan, southbound Bakerloo, northbound Bakerloo, northbound Metropolitan, Up (southbound) LNER and Down (northbound) LNER (the last two are not electrified and are mostly ignored in this description). There are five intermediate stations, none new.

West Hampstead station is in a short cutting and consists of an island platform between the Bakerloo tracks; this had to be shifted northwards as there was no room to slew three tracks south to bring the northbound Bakerloo to its south side. In doing so, a new waiting room was added in the 'Streamline Moderne' style, with rounded ends and an overhanging canopy. The station is sometimes used as a terminus for northbound trains and so has a siding between the tracks just to the north to allow them to reverse. The ticket hall is at street level, reached by stairs up from the platform and is a wide two-storey brick building with the entrance at one side due to the shift. Two other railways are roughly parallel at

Streamline Moderne waiting room at Kilburn.

this point and the three stations are less than 180m (600ft) apart along the road.

Kilburn is immediately west of a set of road bridges, each carrying two tracks over a road junction, meaning that moving any of them would be a major job. As it was, there were platforms on the two slow lines. The southbound slow platform was widened to reach the northbound fast – these two became the Bakerloo tracks – while the northbound slow platform was abandoned and subsequently removed. A Streamline Moderne waiting room was also added here. The booking hall is tucked into the gap between two of the bridges and is best described as bland. In contrast, the bridges themselves are now a bright light blue with 'Metropolitan Railway' and the date 1914 (when the line was widened) spelled out.

Willesden Green has platforms on all four lines, so no change was required; indeed, the platform buildings are the originals from when the station first opened. The two outside platforms – on the Metropolitan tracks – are disused, though the staff maintain gardens on them. As part of the conversion work a reversing siding was added at the north end of this station as well. From here, the line starts a long descent towards Neasden. The two-storey station building on the road above was built

in 1925. It was designed by the railway's architect Charles Clark, is faced in white marble with the company and station name in bold black letters beneath the roofline, and has one of his characteristic diamond-shaped clocks jutting out from the wall. Inside the booking hall, the walls of green tiles in various shades and solid wooden frames around the ticket windows have survived mostly unchanged.

Dollis Hill station is the newest of the five, having opened in 1909. Like West Hampstead, the island platform had to be moved north by one track and it also gained a Streamline Moderne waiting room. At street level there is no station at all. Instead, the booking office is under the tracks with subways to the streets on either side. The long passageways are now decorated with images of old maps of the area overlaid with classical-style star maps.

The last of the five stations is Neasden. This also had platforms on all four tracks and so needed no change, though in this case the disused platforms are bare. At surface level is a single-storey version of the brick building at West Hampstead, though with the entrance central.

On the north side of the line between Neasden and Wembley Park can be found Neasden Depot and Works. For well over a century this has been

Original mosaics and wooden detail mix with modern additions at Willesden Green.

Decorations in the subway to Dollis Hill station.

the Metropolitan's main storage place for trains and the depot for maintenance and engineering works, and after a major rebuild completed in 1938 it was in a position to take over this work for the Bakerloo as well, allowing London Road and Queen's Park depots to be downgraded to their present role as storage sidings. Neasden depot had an eight-road shed for examinations and a four-road shed for cleaning, plus two three-road double-length sheds for detailed inspection and repairs. It was also fitted with the latest gadget: a washing machine that could clean a train as it was slowly driven through it. The sheds and sidings could hold 728 cars in total.

Previously, the depot was connected to the line at either end by flat junctions on to the fast tracks, with crossovers to the other pair on the far side of each station. But major changes were made as part of the rearrangement for the Bakerloo. The connection at the Neasden end is still on the flat, but could now reach all four tracks (access from the northbound Metropolitan has since been removed). At the Wembley Park end there is a level connection with both southbound tracks, while a new diveunder emerges between the northbound Metropolitan and Bakerloo tracks, allowing non-conflicting access to either.

Wembley Park station required relatively little change, though one bay platform got moved west and became a through one. Initially the Bakerloo shared tracks with slow Metropolitan trains between the station and the divergence to Stanmore, but this turned out to be an operational nightmare and in 1954 the two were separated, meaning a total of eight tracks between these points. As already stated, the flat junction for the Stanmore branch was replaced by a diveunder passing beneath the southbound Metropolitan tracks.

The branch itself is a simple line that is mostly on embankments. It starts with a 90-degree turn to the north-east, then curves back to the north before the first station of Kingsbury. This was built at Gore Farm, about 800m (half a mile) west of the village of Kingsbury Green, in a cutting under the road. All three original stations on the branch were designed by Charles Clark; this one is a long building in 'cottage' style with the booking office in the centre and spaces for three or four shops on each side. The sloping roof is tall enough to have apartments inside, which were initially used by staff. From there, the line follows the path of Honeypot Lane, though about 200–300m (approximately 200–350 yards) to the east. Plans were made for a second station near the small industrial estate on Honeypot Lane and due west of the housing about to be built on the recently closed Stag Lane aerodrome; this eventually opened about two years after the rest of the branch. With open fields in the area, the station started as a simple wooden halt, but in 1936 this was replaced by a taller version of the Kingsbury station with three floors, not one, of accommodation above it and designed this time by Stanley Heaps. Stretching out from each end of this is a three-storey parade of shops and apartments more than 200m (660ft) long, with a large grassed park area between them and a huge 'UNDERGROUND' roundel impaled on a concrete mast and dish, in turn mounted on a grassy mound. With no obvious name for the site (Honeypot Lane was too long and Stag Lane came nowhere near it), somebody eventually decided that it should be 'Queensbury' to go with 'Kingsbury'.

From here, the line extends almost straight north, still paralleling Honeypot Lane and its extension Marsh Lane, until it reaches London Road about 800m (half a mile) to the east of the original village centre and somewhat less from the present one. There is one intermediate station where the line crosses over Whitchurch Lane, named after the Canons Park estate which it sat on and which was just being opened up for development. The station is an obscure one built into one of the bridge abutments, but inside there are dramatically walled staircases leading up to the platforms. At Stanmore itself the line is heading into the side of a hill and the booking hall is more than 8m (26ft) above the platforms in a narrower version of the Kingsbury station building, in turn sited on a layby set back from the road. The station itself has three platforms and there are ten stabling sidings on the east side.

A train departs Queensbury past the massive station building and the dramatic roundel, but the actual entrance is almost invisible.

The initial peak Bakerloo service was 7tph from Stanmore and a further 7tph from Wembley Park. The Stanmore branch service, running directly to the West End, soon became crowded, par- ticularly because the original plan to have some Metropolitan trains stop at the three stations on the original route soon degenerated into a few peak-hour trains and then stopped entirely.

CHAPTER 9

World War II

War Breaks Out

As well as the opening of the Stanmore branch, 1939 saw the start of World War II. Even before the war, plans were being made. For the Bakerloo, the single biggest concern was – as in 1917 – the possibility of a bomb exploding on the river bed, penetrating the tunnels and flooding much of the line. On 27 September 1938, with the Sudeten crisis in full swing, the line was closed south of Piccadilly Circus and the line plugged with concrete at various places. After Chamberlain's 'peace in our

time' agreement and an apparent end to the risk of a pan-European war, the plugs were drilled out and services resumed on 8 October. One lesson that was learned from the experience is that it wasn't practical to reverse every train using only the southbound platform at Piccadilly Circus and so the emergency crossover was upgraded to a scissors. The same was done north of Lambeth North where the London Road access tunnel joins the line.

However, it was clear to the authorities that this might not be the end of things and so more precautions were put in place. In particular, in early

The chamber containing the crossover for reversing trains at Piccadilly Circus. This is the only place on the Bakerloo that both platform tunnels are visible at the same time.

The frame for floodgate 5 at Embankment; the gate is behind the wall to the right. The red sign is a 'STOP' instruction to drivers going the wrong way.

1939 six floodgates were installed in the tunnels, numbers 1 and 2 at the north end of Embankment station, 5 and 6 at the south end, and 9 and 10 at the north end of Waterloo station (odd numbers were in the northbound tunnel; the missing numbers were on the Northern Line). These were 13in (33cm) thick and had a mass of about 6 tonnes; steel seals with rubber linings were used to fill the gaps where the rails went. They could be closed electrically in under a minute, or by hand if the power was cut. They were interlocked with the signals, but this was to prevent a train being driven into them and would not stop a train being trapped under the river. They would be closed during air raids, requiring the service to be split. Smaller flood doors were also installed in some passageways, typically swinging down from the ceiling of the platform to block the entire entrance. The Northern Line floodgates at Embankment were not ready at the start of the war and so the Bakerloo platforms were closed for just under three months until they were fin-

ished. There were also concerns that stations could be flooded by broken sewers or water mains following a bomb hit. Most could be modified to mitigate the risk without affecting public access, but Maida Vale was closed and surface access at Oxford Circus blocked (it was still possible to change to and from the Central Line) to allow them to be made safe. They reopened after a few months in January and November respectively.

As the Germans invaded Poland on 1 September 1939, all railways in the country were placed under government control, where they would remain throughout the war and beyond. Initially, a complex income-sharing arrangement was put in place. The government would take all the income from fares and pay a proportion (varying with the total) to each of the five operators (the 'Big Four' and the LPTB). Fares were put up by about 10 per cent. From the start of 1941 this was replaced by flat payments – £4,835,705 p.a. for the Underground. None of the railways received enough to meet their

A floodgate being tested during construction. HALCROW

running costs, let alone pay out the dividends that shareholders expected, and as a result the network would suffer from lack of maintenance over the war years.

For the Bakerloo passenger there were few immediate effects. On the first few days of September northbound trains were filled by Operation *Pied Piper*: children, mothers with babies and other evacuees being carried to Harrow or Watford to catch a train to their new home. Non-stopping trains on the Watford route ceased on 16 November, slowing down some journeys. Overall passenger numbers dropped dramatically on all lines, on average to about three-quarters of the pre-war numbers, though they would start to pick up in 1942. Blackout arrangements were put in place: the lighting on trains was replaced by a few

dim blue bulbs, though later some reading lights were added, which the guard could turn off on the surface sections during air raids. Train windows were fitted with a kind of sticky netting to prevent broken glass flying everywhere after a nearby explosion. In 1940, female staff reappeared, initially as porters and ticket collectors.

Sheltering in the Tubes

A major concern of the LPTB, based on memories of the chaos during the Zeppelin raids of the last war, was the use of tube stations as air-raid shelters. Initially, people were banned from sheltering in stations as the authorities were concerned about a 'shelter mentality', with London's population turning into a tribe of troglodytes that never saw the light of day. However, eventually it was realized that there is no way to distinguish a shelterer from a passenger with a 1d ticket who isn't in a hurry and, in October 1940, proper arrangements were brought into effect and would continue until the morning of 7 May 1945.

Much has been written about the tube shelters and it would be redundant to repeat it all here. Shelter spaces were marked out on the platform and tickets issued each day, though regulars would try to reserve their usual space. Chemical toilets and bunk beds were installed and food was pro-

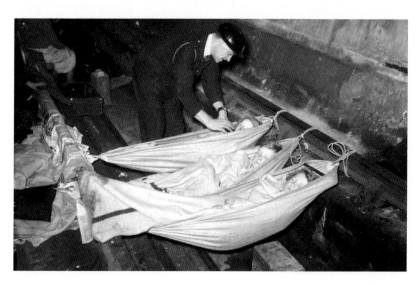

Children sleep in hammocks over the 'suicide' pit; probably at Aldwych or Bethnal Green.

Shelterers sleep on stopped escalators.

vided. From early December 1940 the Bakerloo had a regular food train that carried 7 tonnes of refreshments in about fifty containers. It would run between service trains in the middle of the day, delivering full containers and collecting the empties in the time it would normally take passengers to alight and board. The food would then be warmed at each station and handed out for supper and then breakfast. Eventually all seventeen stations south of Queen's Park and Finchley Road were available for sheltering.

As well as members of the public, various organizations used tube stations for safety. In the case of the Bakerloo, it was Paddington station: GWR's traffic-control staff occupied offices deep down where they would be safe if the main-line station was hit. Occasionally stations got unusual uses. The tale is told of a wedding in 1940 where the celebrations were interrupted by an air-raid warning, so the entire party decamped to Edgware Road station to continue. At the end, the bride and groom were invited to occupy one of the lifts for the night, with the stationmaster stopping it halfway down the shaft to ensure their privacy, if not comfort.

Watford

Returning briefly to the Watford end of the line, the war brought tube trains to the southern side of the Watford triangle, though not in service. Over the interwar years the curve had lost most of its services and by the outbreak of war there were only seven LMSR trains each way per day in the peaks, southbound in the morning and northbound in the evening, running between Croxley Green and a mixture of Euston and Broad Street. In 1941, thirteen of these were cut, leaving a sole Croxley Green to Euston morning peak train. The Bakerloo made up for this by terminating some late morning services at Harrow & Wealdstone, the trains then running empty over the curve to Croxley Green depot; the process was reversed in the early afternoon. This would continue for many years after the war.

The Later War Years

In the later parts of the war period passenger numbers started to grow again and by 1944 they were ahead of pre-war figures. Many of these journeys were being made by newcomers to the network – such as troops passing through – and they could easily get lost or confused in the crowded stations. Escalators were a particular problem: small 'stand on the right' signs had been placed beside the escalators for many years, but in 1944 it was felt necessary to supplement the ones at Piccadilly Circus and Waterloo with large banners. Loudspeakers were installed on busy platforms to help direct people around, but it was to be decades before the strange acoustics of platform tunnels were really overcome. London Transport also introduced its own propaganda characters: Billy Brown and Susan Sensible were the perfect travellers, always doing the right thing and never delaying trains by such activities as blocking the doorways. Little poems would appear; for example, one to discourage people from damaging the window netting ended:

I trust you'll pardon my correction,
That stuff is there for your protection.

to which one wit added the response:

Thank you for the information,
I'd like to see the bloody station.

In August 1944, another ghost of the Zeppelins returned to haunt the Bakerloo. Routine checks had found that the armoured protection installed in the tunnels under the Thames had badly decayed: in particular the concrete had turned to slurry, new concrete (expensive in wartime) was not surviving more than a week, and the longitudinal timbers were starting to rot. The only answer was to completely replace the trackbed and track along the relevant sections. The tunnels were undersized because of the protection and there was no room for mechanical equipment, so everything had to be done with hand machinery. The service was cut back to Piccadilly Circus once again and, in case something went wrong, the floodgates at the north end of Embankment station were closed and a temporary waterproof wall installed at the south end of

Waterloo. The remnants of the concrete were dug out, the plating below the window line cut away with torches, and a new concrete trackbed installed. The whole thing required an eleven-day closure, which German news blamed on a V1 hit.

Death and Damage on the Bakerloo

Though this piece of disruption was home-grown, enemy action did disrupt the Bakerloo. Of the nine hits on the tube system that killed or injured people, the Bakerloo suffered two. At 20:52 on 12 October 1940, a 250kg (550lb) bomb penetrated the road south of Nelson's Column, detonating just above the ticket hall of Trafalgar Square station. The blast damaged fourteen or fifteen of the rings of the lower escalator chamber, three of which collapsed and allowed a large amount of debris to fall in, killing three men and four women and injuring thirty-three others. There was trivial damage to the northbound platform and minor damage to the southbound. Services resumed in the morning with a 10mph (16km/h) speed limit, though it was 11 November before repairs were completed. This was the second hit on the line the same day: at about 19:30 a bomb hit one of the tunnels immediately north of Kensal Green station.

A few months later, at 03:45 on 16 January, an 1,800kg (4,000lb) bomb hit Lambeth North station and badly damaged the southern end of the southbound platform tunnel; around fifty tunnel segments were bulging alarmingly (thirty-seven had to be completely replaced). Twenty shelterers were injured (some sources claim twenty-eight; there is probably no way to resolve the discrepancy at this late stage), with Robert Garland dying of his injuries on 31 January. The northbound and the link to London Road also suffered minor damage. The service had to be curtailed at Waterloo for the next three months. For the first five days, trains reversed at Piccadilly Circus while a shuttle ran between Waterloo and Trafalgar Square, but on 21 January it became possible to use the Lambeth North scissors to reverse trains, though passengers

Crater of the bomb that damaged Trafalgar Square station on 12 October 1940.

were still required to alight at Waterloo. It was 21 April before the line was fully reopened.

Several other stations were also hit. Damage to the tube station building at Marylebone provided a pretext to dust off a 1937 plan and build new escalators from the main-line station to the platforms. The original connecting passage was closed in 1941 and the booking hall moved to the main station. The new station opened on 1 February 1943, with the old one closed and eventually demolished. Between stations, 20m (70ft) of the northbound viaduct at Kilburn was demolished by a bomb in September 1940; temporary repairs were quick, but permanent ones took months. London Road depot was bombed more than once, with the workshops destroyed and the depot effectively downgraded to a stabling point.

The Bakerloo probably had the most surface mileage of all the tube lines at the start of the war, though the Northern was trying to catch up. The problem with surface running, of course, is the weather, particularly frost and snow, which result in an insulating layer of ice on the current rails. In 1940, the Underground introduced sleet locomotives, which were basically a pair of old motored cars with extra bogies carrying brushes and de-icer sprays. These then ran along the lines on particularly cold nights to keep the current rails clear. This of course meant keeping the power on, which prevented routine maintenance. In 1944, the Stanmore branch was used as the testbed for de-icing baths. These were baths full of a de-icing fluid placed in gaps in the current rails every 400–800m (one-quarter to one-half of a mile). A roller in the bath

London Road depot in 1972. The building on the right was bombed in World War II. R.J. GREENAWAY/LURS COLLECTION 01442

transferred the fluid to the bottom of the collector shoes on the train, which then spread it along the rails to keep them clear.

The war ended with the Underground carrying more traffic than ever, though it was not making a profit from it. On the Bakerloo, Stanmore had become so busy that the originally planned peak split of 23:17 between the two branches had to be changed to 20:20 or, rather, 18:18, because the third platform at Elephant & Castle needed for the full service had never been built. But perhaps the peacetime would change that.

CHAPTER 10

1950s, 60s and 70s

Post-War

The war may have ended but the railways remained under state control. But now that people weren't fighting the war anymore, they could concentrate on repairing the damage and returning to a peacetime existence. Not that things would remain the same: in July 1945 the Labour party under Clement Attlee won a general election, crushing the Conservatives under Churchill with a majority of 146.

Part of the new government's platform was the nationalization of key industries, including transport. A British Transport Commission (BTC) was formed and took power on 1 January 1948. A total of fifty-nine railway companies were nationalized. Most of them were merged to form British Railways (BR), but the LPTB and some related operations became the remit of the new London Transport Executive (LTE). In each case, shareholders lost their shares in – and so influence on – the company, being compensated with 'British Transport Stock', a government security traded on the stock market. The shares were converted at 1946 prices, so that LPTB 'B' stock went at £128 3s 9d per £100, while the riskier 'C' stock was only valued at £67 3s 9d. Lord Ashfield was appointed as a full-time member of the BTC, but on 4 November 1948 he died, bringing an end to forty years of running transport in London.

There had been some thinking about the peace even in wartime. Assorted reports on what to do about the railways in London appeared in 1943, 1944 and 1946. But the key one was a BTC document

Lord Ashfield's house in Mayfair (inset: detail of blue plaque).

that was completed in late 1948 and handed to the Minister on 1 February 1949. This proposed ten new tube railways, labelled A to L (there was no route I, and routes J and K were alternatives rather than separate lines). The proposal totalled 165.3 route-km (102¾ route-miles) in length and would cost £238 million. The ones that would be immediately important for the Bakerloo were Route F and Route H, though Route C will come up later in this chapter and Route D in the next. Route F was a main-line sized tunnel route from Kilburn to the Lewisham area via Marylebone, Marble Arch, Trafalgar Square, Aldwych, Ludgate Circus, Bank and Fenchurch Street. If it had been built, the Bakerloo's Watford branch would have been cut back to Harrow & Wealdstone. Route H, on the other hand, was the old staple of extending the Bakerloo to Camberwell, possibly continuing to Herne Hill in the future. The basic route was the same as the 1930 plan and there would be two stations, at Walworth Road and Camberwell Green. Work was supposed to start in January 1950. But in September that year it was announced that the cost had gone up and the project was being 'deferred',

which actually meant killed, though the powers continued to be kept alive.

The Fifties

There were minor improvements during the 1950s. In September 1945, Stonebridge Park station managed to catch fire again and was rebuilt in a modern style during 1948. In 1951, two more escalators were added at Embankment, connecting the ticket hall to the lower concourse. For many years one had a glass side, allowing passengers on the eastbound District Line platform to see the workings. Waterloo gained a new entrance on the west side of York Road in 1951, with three escalators down to the main part of the station. In 1955, one of these was 'borrowed' to go to Green Park, being replaced by fixed stairs. Two years later the entrance was closed to allow the Shell Centre to be constructed around it, reopening in 1962. The original Carpenders Park station, built to serve a golf course, had become overwhelmed by commuters as houses sprang up – covering the golf course *en route* – and by 1937 it was seeing 200,000

York Road entrance to Waterloo.

WATERLOO UNDERGROUND STATION

passengers a year. A new station was built about 200m (660ft) south of the old one, opening in late 1952. By 1957 it was handling 1,300,000 passengers a year.

In 1956, Baker Street became the location for the trial of a power-saving arrangement on 'up' escalators. The escalators would run at half speed when not in use; when a passenger stepped on, they speeded up for the length of time it would take to ride to the top, then slowed down again if nobody else had boarded. (An earlier version of this had been in use elsewhere since 1934, but the Baker Street version was simpler and better.) Eventually forty-six escalators around the network would be fitted with this device, but they were abandoned in 1974 when it was determined that they were not cost-effective.

The Sixties

Politicians, having taken control of public transport, weren't happy to leave it alone. In the early 1960s, the Conservatives under Harold Macmillan were concerned about the financial problems that the BTC was suffering and decided to break it up into five separate bodies. The London Transport Executive went with it, to be replaced by one of the five – the London Transport Board – on 1 January 1963. However, this was not a mere renaming. The LTB reported directly to the Minister for Transport, who appointed its members and controlled the purse strings. It turned out to be £161,830,904 in debt at its creation and was told to pay a smidgeon over £5.5 million a year in interest as well as eventually repaying it.

While 'Supermac' was reorganizing the structure, the planners were about to make the biggest change to London's transport in sixty years: Route C of the 1949 plan was going ahead. The original Route C was a tube line that would run from Angel Road station (replaced by Meridian Water station in 2019) via Finsbury Park, Euston, Oxford Circus, Brixton and Streatham to East Croydon; there might be branches to Walthamstow and towards Enfield. During the 1950s there were proposals to divert the southern end to Wimbledon. The new line would reduce demand for the Bakerloo, which meant that Route H could be revived to extend the Bakerloo to Camberwell Green with a 40tph service. However, the overall costs of this plan (including a new depot at Stanmore) soon killed it. But the main Route C was to go ahead, though with only the Walthamstow branch and no Angel Road, under its new name of the Victoria Line. Walthamstow to Victoria was authorized in December 1961 and the section from there to Brixton in August 1967.

The Victoria Line crosses the Bakerloo at one point: Oxford Circus station, where cross-platform interchange was intended. This meant that the station would need to be rebuilt *again*, this time on a grand scale. The station was already over-crowded, which meant that this expansion had to be done without interrupting the daily use. The decision was made to build a brand new ticket hall under the road junction itself, with escalators down to the north end of the Bakerloo and Victoria Lines (the Victoria Line tubes are outside the Bakerloo ones, with cross-passages between the platform tunnels in the same direction); there are separate flights for the northbound and southbound platforms. There was no possibility of closing the junction for years, so a steel 'umbrella' – effectively a massive bridge – was put in place over it on the Bank Holiday weekend of 3–5 August 1963. Work could then be done underneath without disturbing the traffic. In the 4½ years it stood there (it was removed over the Easter weekend of 1968) it carried some 44 million vehicles without mishap. The existing station remained in use to serve the Central Line and the south end of the Bakerloo and Victoria Lines and new linking passages were built. The Victoria Line started serving the rebuilt station on 7 March 1969. Although the new line would relieve the Bakerloo between Waterloo and Oxford Circus, it actually generated more traffic north of the latter, increasing the congestion on an already busy section.

Outside Oxford Circus the decade saw more minor improvements. In 1963, the Marylebone escalator shaft and concourse tunnels were finally completed, having been 'under construction' for nearly twenty years. The next year Stanmore gained a new ticket office at platform level for car park users (the car park is lower than the road and users previously had to walk upstairs to the station entrance and then down again). Also in 1964 South Kenton gained a public subway under the line to replace the unusually high footbridge, which had been a source of complaint since well before the war. On the other hand, the train indicator for southbound trains broke down in September of the same year, to be replaced by a notice explaining that the red trains went to Elephant & Castle, while the green ones went to Euston or Broad Street (mostly the former). The following year Lambeth North got a new ticket office, replacing the passimeter. The long embankments on the Stanmore branch, particularly the older ones south of Wembley Park, are always in danger of slipping down. In 1965, an ongoing programme was started to stabilize them, usually by injecting cement grout under pressure deep into the embankment to form solid piles that prevent a slip. Waterloo gained more escalators in 1967; the work was particularly difficult because of unstable ground and the cramped layout where the shaft was driven.

On 16 November 1965 there was an unusual 'strike' by passengers at Queen's Park. The services to Watford had, by this stage, been reduced to the peak hours only and a power failure had affected the BR service from Euston. About 1,000 passengers refused to get off the train, which was supposed to reverse in the sheds at the north end, demanding that it continued to Watford instead. Before things could get too nasty, a BR train finally arrived and was no doubt overwhelmed by the desperate commuters.

Camberwell remained an ongoing obsession in some quarters and 1965 saw another plan launched to extend the Bakerloo there. Camberwell itself was not justifiable on commercial grounds, but if the line went all the way to Peckham that would allow British Rail services in the area to be reduced, which might cover the losses. Between 1969 and 1974, the plan was put together in detail, but it still did not look good. It was then referred to the London Rail Plan of 1974, which concluded that there were higher priorities, ending that attempt.

Services were run down a bit during the 1960s, though not consistently; for example, cuts in 1964 were restored in 1967, then new cuts were introduced in the summer of 1968, reversed the

View over Watford as a train approaches Bushey from the Colne Viaduct. LURS COLLECTION 01406

following spring, then more cuts were made next autumn. More importantly, in June 1965 the off-peak service on the Watford branch was eliminated completely north of Queen's Park and the peak service was reduced to merely ten southbound trains in the morning and northbound in the evening: six Watford and four Harrow. In October, two of the Watford trains were removed and four years later all the Harrow trains disappeared. Another change on the Watford branch, though only marginally affecting the Bakerloo, was that the curve from Bushey to Croxley Green depot was closed in 1966, meaning that trains had to run to the depot via Watford High Street.

The Seventies

Politics struck again in 1969. The Greater London Council (GLC) had been created in 1965 and in 1968 it was decided to give it control of transport in London. The GLC insisted that the LTB's debts should be written off and new policies were put together that allowed national government to fund infrastructure improvements rather than finding the money out of fares. And so, on the first day of the 1970s, the London Transport Board was replaced by the London Transport Executive, a body of the GLC.

One of the first things to happen under the LTE was to change the electrification system of the Watford branch to be compatible with the other main-line railways. The original LNWR electrification reached to Richmond and, at about the same time, the LSWR had electrified the main route through there on the third-rail system. In August 1970, all the ex-LNWR lines were converted to the latter. In places where Underground trains also ran, the central fourth rail was left in place but bonded to the running rails – this meant that trains equipped for either system received the correct voltage – whereas elsewhere the fourth rail was either removed, or taken off its insulators and left in the 'four foot' (the space between the running rails) as an extra path for the return current. On the Watford branch this meant that the fourth rail con-

tinued to be in place from Queen's Park to Watford Junction and as far as Croxley Green depot, though not to Croxley Green station. In addition, it was left in place from Queen's Park to Kilburn High Road, the next station on the DC lines to Euston. The reason for this was that a southbound Bakerloo Line train might not be able to be routed on to the Underground lines at Queen's Park for some reason. Such trains could (and still can) run to Kilburn High Road, then reverse over the crossover and back north to Queen's Park, where they can re-enter service northbound. (Until 1988 the crossover was at the south end of the station; it is now at the north end.)

Other minor works were carried out in the 1970s. The wooden northbound platform at Queensbury had to be rebuilt in 1973–4 because it was showing a distressing preference to be at the bottom of the embankment rather than the top where it belonged. However, this was really only a stopgap and both Queensbury and Canons Park platforms were replaced by concrete ones in 1979. In 1976, there were modifications to the ticket hall at Embankment in order to give more public space.

The 1970s were a time of Provisional IRA terrorist attacks, particularly in London. The Bakerloo Line was affected three times, on 23 and 30 August 1973 at Baker Street and on 13 February 1976 at Oxford Circus. In each case a carrier bag or case containing a bomb was left in the ticket hall (or on a footbridge in the case of the second Baker Street bomb), timed to go off in the evening rush hour. Each time the bomb was spotted and defused by police experts shortly before it could detonate. Both Baker Street bombs were small, while the 1976 bomb is reported as containing 9kg (20lb) of explosives and packed with bolts to generate large amounts of shrapnel. As a result of these and other attacks, litter bins were removed from all Underground stations, not to return for many years.

The 1970s were also a period of financial crisis and high inflation (it was also in 1971 when shillings and old pence were finally put to rest, replaced by decimal currency with 100 new pence in a pound). In this period there were ten

A special railtour using 1938 Stock reverses at Kilburn High Road; the rust on the negative rail shows the lack of use. R.J. GREENAWAY/ LURS COLLECTION 04195

price rises totalling 436 per cent, or just under 16 per cent per annum; in the middle of the decade there were three increases in sixteen months totalling 212 per cent. It is perhaps not surprising that demand decreased on the Underground. The average drop was about 3.8 per cent per annum, though this hides significant increases in 1977 and 1978, probably due to increased tourism during and just after the Queen's Silver Jubilee. However, GLC policy was to keep the trains running, so there weren't service cuts to match; rather, train-kilometres grew about 5.6 per cent between 1972 and 1981. One interesting protest against fare increases took place in 1977: protesters would buy a 10p ticket on entry to the system and, at their destination, would hand in the ticket, their name and address, and an IOU for the balance, meaning that London Transport would have to go through some effort to get the rest of its money. However, the courts decided that this constituted an attempt to avoid payment and protesters could be prosecuted accordingly.

Meanwhile, the Bakerloo was preparing for its next big upheaval.

CHAPTER 11

Jubilee and Beyond

The Jubilee Line

The Victoria Line had opened in stages between 1968 and 1971 and showed that new tube lines could be a success and a benefit to London. Planners therefore started (or continued) looking at options for more tube lines to build.

Back in 1965 a plan had been put together for railways in London that included extending two tube lines and building a new one. The new 'Fleet Line' was a combination of parts of routes D and F from the 1949 plan and would run from Baker Street to meet the gap that separates the Central and District Lines, where it would run east along the Strand, Fleet Street and Cannon Street to reach BR's Fenchurch Street station and then cross the Thames to take over or run along the southern part of the East London Line.

At the same time, the planners had realized that adding the Stanmore branch to the Bakerloo Line had been a mistake. While it had seemed necessary at the time for reasons already described, the problem was that the branches joined too close to the central section, arguably within it. So many people were using the Stanmore branch that it had had to take over more of the 'slots' into central London than had been planned, which in turn meant that there could not be enough trains on the Watford branch to satisfy demand. Ideally,

the branches should have met at somewhere like Queen's Park or Kilburn, but, of course, it was far too late for that. Since the Fleet Line would need to head into the suburbs at its western end, it made a lot of sense and would cost almost nothing for it to take over the Stanmore branch.

The final route was split into four stages, each with its own Act of Parliament. Stage I ran from Stanmore to Baker Street, then Bond Street, Green Park and Trafalgar Square, with the tunnels extending most of the way to Aldwych; Parliamentary powers were sought and granted in 1969 (the authority ends at 148 Strand, though the tunnels apparently end at number 111). Stage II went from Aldwych (where the 1965 plan also suggested extending the Piccadilly branch to Waterloo) and ran to Fenchurch Street with stations at Ludgate Circus and Cannon Street, while Stage III then took it under the Thames to Surrey Docks (now called Surrey Quays), where it would take over the East London Line tracks to New Cross and New Cross Gate (in those days there was no connection to Peckham). The Acts for both of these received Royal Assent in 1971. Finally, Stage IV continued the New Cross branch to Lewisham along existing BR tracks; this Act was approved the following year. Initial work on Stage I started in 1970 and the full cost for it was made available the following year.

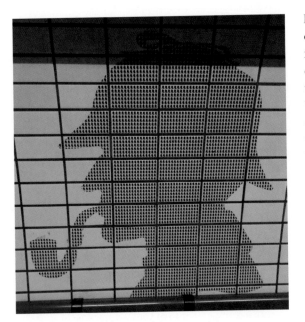

Decoration at Baker Street: Sherlock Holmes made up of about 2,700 Sherlock Holmeses.

As can be seen, the Fleet Line crosses the Bakerloo at two places: Baker Street and Trafalgar Square. At Baker Street there was already a separate southbound platform on the Stanmore branch that could form the starting point of the new south/eastbound tunnel. However, there would obviously need to be a new northbound platform. This was built above the southbound and on the same level as the Bakerloo's existing northbound with cross-passages between them, so that the existing escalators could be used and passengers had easy interchanges in both directions. The tunnel then meets the existing northbound Stanmore branch just where it crosses Boston Place. In both directions the existing links into the Bakerloo tracks were retained so that trains could be moved between the lines as necessary. Both junctions had to be built without disturbing the Bakerloo traffic. The junction tunnels were built around the existing tubes, which were then dismantled at night. All four platforms were decorated with a Sherlock Holmes theme.

Trafalgar Square was both an easier job and a much more complicated one: no track connections were needed, but various passenger ones were. The Fleet Line tunnels pass underneath the Bakerloo at about 45 degrees and the Northern Line's Charing Cross branch at right angles about 200m (660ft) apart, meaning that it made sense to put the new platforms between the two and combine the existing stations (Trafalgar Square and Strand) into one new one, which was named Charing Cross. At the Strand end the booking hall was expanded and a new flight of three escalators was dug from there, passing through the old lift shafts, to just above the level of the existing station. At both ends a second flight of three was built from

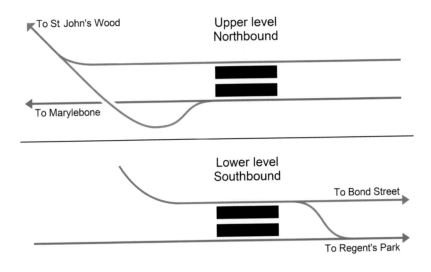

Layout of Baker Street tube station from 1979 onwards.

A Sherlock Holmes story – in this case, 'The Red-Headed League' – above a seat .

the bottom of the escalators (existing ones for the Bakerloo) down to the Fleet Line level. A long horizontal foot tunnel was also built between the two intermediate levels.

While the Fleet Line's takeover of the Stanmore branch would bring benefits to the Bakerloo, it also introduced a serious problem. The only major depot on the line was at Neasden – Queen's Park, Croxley Green and London Road were not up to the job – and that would no longer be on the line, nor would there be the capacity to run trains to and from there. That meant a new depot was needed. The death of the Peckham proposal eliminated the possibility of a depot there, so where to put it? The answer came from an unexpected direction: the original New Lines project received its electricity from a power station close to Stonebridge Park, but this had closed in 1967.

If it were to be demolished, there would be a nice big space available right next to a line that the Bakerloo ran along. Therefore an agreement was reached to take over the space and build a major new depot there, one that is now the Bakerloo's only real depot. It has fourteen roads in two separate buildings plus three others in the open air, each capable of holding a train. The approach tracks are laid out and signalled so that trains can reverse in them clear of the running lines without having to occupy depot space. Significant automation was added from the start, with CCTV supervision of the tracks and a train washer that operated as soon as a train drove into it. There are operational restrictions on the depot because of planning restrictions imposed after petitions from nearby residents, even though the line had been there long before their houses.

A Bakerloo train waits for a Watford to Euston train to pass before entering the running line from Stonebridge Park depot.

In 1977, control of the GLC changed hands and the new Conservative administration announced that it was changing the name of the Fleet Line to the Jubilee Line. The justifications seem flimsy: celebrating the Queen's Silver Jubilee might have made more sense if the line had actually opened in 1977. But the change went ahead anyway; LT apparently had to spend £50,000 to change signs and other paperwork.

The Jubilee Line, as we must now call it, finally opened as far as Trafalgar Square on 1 May 1979. Once it had opened, the Bakerloo service could be ramped up and became 24tph in the morning peak, 22tph in the evening peak (which is typically more spread out), 16tph between the peaks, and 12tph in the evenings and Saturdays. Normally northbound Bakerloo trains terminated at Queen's Park, but this could not handle all the reversals in the peaks, so 7 or 8tph continued to Stonebridge Park in service, then reversed in the depot approach tracks. The four 'tidal' trains from and to Watford Junction also continued. Because most Bakerloo services ran entirely in tunnel, the Bakerloo and Jubilee shared

drivers for some years so that they all got time in the open air. The split was successful; within six months the number of peak passengers between Baker Street and Oxford Circus, formerly the

THE RIVER LINE

Even as Stage I was being built and powers existed for Stages II to IV, the planners were looking at other options. Many of the London docks were closing as ships became bigger and needed to moor further downstream, meaning that the Docklands area between Tower Bridge and Barking would need a new purpose to stop it becoming a wasteland (the docks had already suffered badly in World War II, with much of the damage still unrepaired).

This led, in the late 1970s, to a new route known as the River Line. This followed Stages II and III of the original Fleet Line as far as Fenchurch Street, but did not cross the Thames at this point. Instead, there would be stations at St Katharine Docks, Wapping, then no fewer than five river crossings as the line went through Surrey Docks, Millwall, North Greenwich, Custom House, Silvertown and Woolwich Arsenal, to two stations in the Thamesmead area (though there were proposals to reduce the number by diverting the Thames, presumably through some of the redundant docks).

Money remained a problem and the River Line died in 1979, though the concept was partly reborn in the Docklands Light Railway.

Trafalgar Square three days before the Jubilee Line opened;
note the new name hiding behind a sticker on the roundel.
DR NEIL CLIFTON

busiest section, had almost halved because of transfers to the Jubilee. Off-peak traffic on both routes started growing.

We must now jump ahead ten years or so. The full story is outside the scope of this book, but the original route of the Jubilee Line was never taken beyond Stage I, with the tunnels to Aldwych remaining unused.

In 1992, the present route of the Jubilee was finally approved, branching off the original line at Green Park, running along the south of the Thames to serve Waterloo and London Bridge stations, before crossing the Thames three more times on its way to Stratford. The section from Green Park to Trafalgar Square was abandoned (though remains available if trains need to be turned round) and the six lower escalators at the latter are boarded up. The long foot passage is still available for those foolish enough to change lines here, or for Bakerloo passengers wanting to avoid the rain on the way to Charing Cross main-line station.

The line now crosses the Bakerloo at Waterloo and major work had to be done there to handle not only the Jubilee Line, but also the Eurostar terminal that opened in 1994 (and closed in 2007). The Jubilee had its own ticket hall on Waterloo Road, but technical reasons meant that the platform tunnels had to be rather far east. Therefore they are joined to the existing Underground station by two moving walkways (which in turn are essentially escalators with no slope) 115.940m (380ft 5in) long. Three new escalators were also added from the booking hall to the existing tube level, making eight plus the three from the Shell Centre.

The Jubilee Line Extension opened in four stages during 1999, starting from the Stratford end. Waterloo became the new terminus of this part on 24 September, with through running (and the closure of the Trafalgar Square route) on 20 November, just in time for the Millennium celebrations.

The blocked-off escalators at the
Northern Line end of the long
passage to Trafalgar Square (on the
right).

The loss of the Stanmore branch to the new Jubilee Line was the last major event that happened to the Bakerloo Line. Since then, it has been a matter of gradual improvements to both facilities and services. As a result, the rest of this chapter is more in thematic order than time order.

Politics

First, there is always politics. We left the line being run by the LTE, controlled by the GLC. The GLC had an election in 1981, which was won by Labour, with Ken Livingstone becoming Mayor. The GLC administration and its policies quickly became a thorn in the side of the Conservative government under Margaret Thatcher (in fact, *no* GLC election was won by the party in control of the national government). Within a few years, the government had decided to abolish the GLC, which happened on 31 March 1986. But as a first stage they pulled away the GLC's biggest single responsibility: the London Transport Executive. The legislation to replace the LTE gained Royal Assent on 26 June 1984 and three days later the new London Regional Transport (LRT) took control from it. The change was so rushed that banks actually froze its accounts because they hadn't received formal notification of the change. On 29 March the next year the LRT created a new company, London Underground Limited, which took over the Underground three days later, on 1 April.

LRT was a national government body and, as such, managed to last longer than its predecessor. However, Labour party policy included reinstatement of a single local authority for the whole of London and so, when in 1997 Labour finally pushed the Conservatives out of power at Westminster, they took steps to create what would be called the Greater London Authority. After elections were held, the GLA formally took power on 3 July 2000, with Ken Livingstone as its directly elected mayor (though as an independent, having broken with the Labour party). On the same date the LRT was abolished, replaced by the new Transport for London; at the time of writing, TfL still controls transport in London.

Despite this, politics would hurt the Underground once more. This Labour government was fiscally much more conservative than previous ones and it decided to effectively privatize the Underground (British Rail had been privatized in 1994). The system would still be owned and services run by TfL, but Public–Private Partnerships (PPP) would provide and maintain the trains, stations and related infrastructure. For this purpose, the network was divided into three parts:

- BCV Bakerloo, Central, Victoria, and Waterloo & City Lines
- JNP Jubilee, Northern, and Piccadilly Lines
- SSL Circle, District, East London, Hammersmith & City, and Metropolitan Lines.

The JNP contract was won by a company called Tube Lines (owned by the three engineering and infrastructure companies Amey, Bechtel and Jarvis) and the other two by Metronet (owned by two engineering and infrastructure companies – Atkins and Balfour Beatty – one train manufacturer – Bombardier – and two utilities – EDF Energy and Thames Water). The companies were awarded thirty-year contracts starting in April 2003.

The PPP system quickly turned into a disaster. Metronet was blamed for an accident on the Central Line in 2004 because it had failed to implement safety checks. After two years, the company had started less than half the planned station refurbishments, replaced only 28km (17 miles) of the planned 48km (30 miles) of track, and was way behind on train refurbishment. Despite this, it had made a profit of over £50 million. There were further criticisms – it later turned out that both companies had been awarding their members contracts at significantly higher prices than competitive tenders would have resulted in – and on 18 July 2007 Metronet went into administration. TfL had to meet a funding shortfall of £2,000 million because the PPP contracts meant that Metronet's backers didn't have to. Just under a year later, on 27 May, the Metronet business – including the Bakerloo Line – was transferred to TfL control and the com-

'Piano keyboard' flooring and projected advertisements on the tunnel wall at Waterloo.

panies wound up. The process had cost the taxpayer somewhere between £170 and £410 million. Since then, TfL has remained under GLA control with all work managed in-house and most of it done there, though major projects are contracted out to specialist companies.

WHAT ABOUT TUBE LINES?

Tube Lines appears to have been run in a better manner than Metronet and provided a generally efficient service over its first few years. However, in 2010 the company was some months behind on its work, then disagreed with TfL over its cost estimates for the next period, an argument it lost at arbitration. Tube Lines claimed to be unable to carry on and on 7 May it was announced that TfL was to buy its entire shareholding, putting the company back under TfL control and ending the PPP experiment.

Fares

Returning to 1981, the new Labour administration at the GLA decided to make major reductions to Underground fares under the title 'Fares Fair'. Prices were decreased by an average of 32 per cent, funded by an increase in rates (property taxes). Much more importantly for the future, though, was that the mileage-based fares system was abolished in the central area (the area bounded by the Circle Line plus six stations just outside it and six stations south of the river). Instead, there were two overlapping zones, called the West End and City zones; seventeen stations were in both. The Bakerloo Line was in the West End zone from Paddington to Lambeth North and the City zone from Trafalgar Square to Elephant & Castle. There was a flat fare of 20p within a zone or 30p to cross both zones (though a few marginal cases were still charged 20p). Fares outside the zones were charged on the old basis plus a 10p or 30p supplement for entering the zones.

The London Borough of Bromley complained that its ratepayers were subsidising this scheme for no benefit (there are no Underground lines there) and won in court, causing fares to be roughly doubled from 21 March 1982, though still using the new zones; the new zonal fares were 40p and 70p. After some legal manoeuvring, a new scheme was introduced on 22 May 1983. This involved five concentric zones: the central zone (a merger of the two old zones) and four others at roughly 5km (3-mile) spacing. Fares were reduced by an average of 25 per cent; the fares were 30p, 50p, 80p, £1 and £1.30 for 1 to 5 zones, respectively, except that the one-zone fare was 40p in the central zone and there were some lower fares for short journeys across zonal boundaries. Over time, there have been adjustments – new zones have been added and the short journey fares abolished – but the system is still in use today.

Changes to Services

One piece of fallout from the fares argument was a need to reduce costs drastically. In early 1982, there were plans to reduce peak-hour services and possibly to close some stations either outside the peaks or totally. On the Bakerloo, Edgware Road and Regent's Park were both on the hit list. However, the unions refused to work the new timetable because of the reduced income for their members. After negotiation, some cuts were agreed. The Watford Junction peak 'tidal' service had been carrying fairly few passengers and, to a large extent, it was only running because the trains needed to get to Croxley Green depot anyway. Now that there was a shiny new depot at Stonebridge Park, this was no longer a factor and that tipped the scales; no Bakerloo trains ran north of Stonebridge Park after 24 September, removing more than half the line in one single stroke and throwing the entire burden on

British Rail. There were complaints from passengers and a survey was done, which found that there was significant traffic from Harrow & Wealdstone, but relatively little demand for direct services from north of there, so on 4 June 1984 peak-hour services were restored to Harrow, but the Bakerloo never went north of there again and the negative rail soon ended up in the 'four foot'. With no Bakerloo trains and the ability for main-line trains to go to many more places, and therefore depots, there was no longer a need for Croxley Green depot and it closed on 2 November 1985.

Meanwhile, Harrow & Wealdstone gained trains all day six days a week in May 1988 and 2tph on Sundays (plus the 2tph of the BR service) a year later. Finally, also in 1988, one of the two sidings at the north end of Harrow station was removed and instead a crossover was added at the south end. This means that one train can reverse in service without having to go into the siding while another is stabled there, though the usual arrangement is for trains to reverse via the siding so that all southbound trains – Bakerloo or main line – depart from the same platform.

Ticketing Systems

Returning to fares, in the last sixty years the Underground has been through several ticketing systems, not including the move to zonal fares. The Victoria Line introduced the idea of gates that could read tickets and thus replace ticket checkers, as well as free-standing machines to sell tickets. These appeared at many stations, but it was found that extending the system was not economically justified. By the early 1980s, security from robbery had become a much greater concern and it was decided to introduce a new scheme called UTS (Underground Ticketing System). All zone 1 stations would have gates and throughout the network ticket machines would be moved into the walls of the booking hall so that they could be serviced and have cash removed from the rear; the free-standing passimeters would be abolished. There were two types of machine: a type

One reversing siding being removed at Harrow & Wealdstone (inset: detail of the shunt signal). LURS COLLECTION 01719/01725

that had a button for every station on the network plus buttons to choose the fare type (single, return, child and so on), and a type that sold the commonest ten tickets. One innovation was that the machines could give change or, if they didn't have enough, would move to an 'exact fare only' mode until staff topped them up from the back. Tickets changed from the small Edmondson size to the credit-card sized ones already in use by British Rail and were compatible with them. The work started in 1986 – the Bakerloo was in the forefront, since the first UTS gates on the network were installed at Regent's Park in October 1987 – and took about five years to complete, though Bank remained unfinished until 1992 because of other work going on there. It was highly disruptive to stations and some had to undergo major modifications to fit everything in.

In 1984, the Underground introduced the Travelcard, which gave unlimited travel on the Underground and buses for a day (except in the morning peaks). This was, in fact, a rebrand-

ing of the Twin Rover that had been available in the 1960s and early 1970s, though the price had gone up from 10/- to £2. This was followed early the next year by the Capitalcard, which added British Rail to the mix. Both were also available in weekly, monthly and annual versions (without the peak restriction). In January 1989, the Capitalcard was renamed the Travelcard, with the non-BR version being abolished, and is still a popular ticket today.

Concerns about valuable period Travelcards being 'eaten' by the gates led to experiments in April 1990 with an electronic tag that could be detected by touching it on a pad on the side of a gate. There seem to have been no attempts to go ahead with this scheme – instead, monthly or longer tickets were issued on flexible plastic and staff were trained in quickly recovering lost tickets – but it can be seen as the predecessor of Oyster.

The Oyster card was introduced in 2003. It is a contactless card that is touched on a pad on a ticket gate on entry to and exit from the system. The

Reused ticket windows at Edgware Road (left) and Kilburn Park.

card can hold electronic period tickets and also electronic money, with the fare deducted from the value on the card when the user exits (the user is prevented from entering if the card doesn't have enough money on it). Money can be added to the card at ticket machines. Some innovations were introduced, such as daily capping – a limit on the amount deducted each day – but these are restricted by the technology used and separate peak and off-peak fares were introduced. Installing Oyster also led to almost all stations having gates added. In 2014, the general availability of contactless credit and debit cards was used to add yet another way to pay: these cards can be tapped on the Oyster pad of a gate to get it to open. Unlike Oyster, where the electronic money is held on the card, these taps are merely reported to a central computer system that, overnight, bills the customer through the normal retail payment network. This system does not suffer the technological limitations of Oyster and it is possible to introduce further innovations such as weekly capping.

By 2015, only 3 per cent of ticket purchases on the Underground involved a ticket office and it was decided to abolish them. The last one to close was on the Bakerloo, at Harlesden, on 17 May 2019. In some places station staff have taken the opportunity to repurpose the ticket windows.

Refurbishments and Changes

The original 1906 lifts have long since been replaced with escalators at most stations, but four Bakerloo stations are quiet enough that the work has never been justified. However, lifts wear out and need replacing or refurbishing. At Regent's Park the work started on one lift in 1982 and the other in 1984, but the replacements were not working until early 1987 and for over two years passengers had to use the emergency staircase.

Decorative lift number sign at Regent's Park.

Users at Lambeth North had a similar need to be fit for a twenty-month period starting in mid-1986. When it came to Edgware Road in 1990, however, the decision was made to close the station for the same length of time (only two of the three lifts were replaced, with the third being removed); the station closed again for almost three weeks in 2001 to repair the new lifts. In all three cases, the lifts lasted nowhere near as long as their predecessors and all three were closed for between seven and eleven months for a second set of replacements (*see* Appendix I for dates). Elephant & Castle managed to have three of its four lifts replaced (and one removed) between 1987 and 1990 without major disruption because there are two separate shafts and because the Northern Line lifts could also be used. Although stations elsewhere have gained new lifts in recent years as more attention is paid to the needs of passengers with mobility problems, the only Bakerloo station to be treated to these so far is Harrow & Wealdstone.

Assorted station upgrades have taken place over the years. In 1983, Trafalgar Square received new platform decorations based on paintings in the nearby art galleries and starting the same year Oxford Circus got a 'people in a maze' theme, though some would say it looks more like interlocking escalators (much of it was lost in a 2007 refurbishment). In 1986, Paddington got tiles carrying pictures of assorted tunnelling machines; more importantly, the station was rearranged so that it was possible to change between the Bakerloo and District Lines without going through ticket gates. In 1988, Waterloo was redecorated with a 'harlequin' mask design and black and white patterns on the floor that look rather like a piano keyboard. Out in the open air, Stonebridge Park and Willesden Junction were rebuilt in 2000. The biggest project, however, was the refurbishment of Piccadilly Circus in the late 1980s, restoring it to the style of the 1920s rebuild while widening the entrance passages and adding new colourful decorations to the platforms.

An old-fashioned train indicator at Elephant & Castle with a 'coffee pot' signal repeater attached to allow the guard to know whether the starting signal was clear. The 'new lifts' poster suggests a date in the late 1980s.
LURS COLLECTION 86HA6

Wall decorations at Trafalgar Square (now Charing Cross) based on royalty in the nearby National Portrait Gallery.

The planners had another go at the Bakerloo in the 1988 Central London Rail Study. This time the attack was two-pronged. At the north end, a new branch would run in tunnel from Queen's Park to North Acton, where it would surface and take over the Central Line branch to Ealing Broadway (the Central needed to lose a branch because it would be taking over the District Line branch to Richmond via a new tunnel from Shepherd's Bush to Turnham Green). At the south end, the line would be extended to New Cross Gate via two new stations, one at the Old Kent Road end of Dunton Road and the other on Rotherhithe New Road just west of South Bermondsey station. It would then either continue in tunnel to Lewisham, or surface and use the existing main line to West Croydon and Crystal Palace (just as the East London Line now does). Neither part of the proposal actually helped the central area and it was quietly buried in the 'further work needed' filing cabinet.

From 20 November 1989 Bakerloo trains lost their guards, with only the driver left on the train to open and close doors as well as their other work. This required better lighting and CCTV to be installed (though mirrors could be used on surface stations). The changeover was generally successful, partly because trains were no longer stopped by the lack of guard even though they had a driver. On the other hand, the higher pay for the extra duties caused a drain of drivers from the lines still with guards, affecting their reliability.

Back in World War I, readers may remember, work was done on the tunnels under the Thames to protect them against bombs, which then had to be redone in World War II. In 1996, it was decided to reinforce them again by lining the affected section of the tunnels with concrete. The work took eight months from November to the following July and the line was closed south of Piccadilly Circus for the duration. During the work a train derailed at

Oxford Circus platform decorations.

Piccadilly Circus and the northbound service had to be suspended for ten days between there and Oxford Circus.

In September 2002, the northbound platforms on both tube lines at Baker Street were closed on weekdays while repairs were made to the escalators, though they were reopened at weekends. In mid-January they were opened on weekday evenings and three weeks later the midday period was added. The closure ended at the start of May. During this period, in late November, all stations only served by lifts were closed for a week because of a strike by firefighters; there was concern about a lift jamming if a station caught on fire. This meant that Waterloo was the south end of the line during this period. In 2014, it was Embankment's turn to have its escalators replaced; the platforms

on both tube lines were closed for ten months. Finally, the early summer of 2016 saw the Bakerloo Line service at Paddington closed for four months. During this time two new escalators were added, starting at a cross-passage between the Bakerloo platforms and descending 6.165m (20ft 3in) to a 150m (500ft) passageway, which eventually emerges behind the gates in the new Elizabeth Line ticket hall.

Elephant & Castle station was refurbished in 2007 and the original platform tiles were covered over. The surface building has been restored in the original Leslie Green style, though with a strange glass prism added on one side to hold a gate line.

The 36tph services of the early days are now a distant memory. In 1999, services were 24tph peak,

The side of Elephant & Castle station.

20tph off-peak and 18tph at weekends, with mostly 6tph to Harrow & Wealdstone, probably the densest it ever was in recent time. By 2007, the peaks were down to 22tph in the morning and 21tph in the evening, though Saturdays were up to 20tph in the afternoons; the Harrow service remained unchanged. Since then, the numbers have remained mostly unchanged, though Saturday 'afternoon' now starts at 07.45 and ends at 23.00. The main-line service between Euston and Watford Junction *has*

increased during this period, from 3tph to 4tph. In the middle of 2019 the Bakerloo Line was operating 11085.88km (6,888 miles 786yd) in passenger service on weekdays, equivalent to 238 round-trip journeys between Elephant & Castle and Harrow & Wealdstone.

The Bakerloo has become a stable operation, with no major changes about to happen, though we never know what the future will bring. Meanwhile, it is time to look at some of the details.

CHAPTER 12

Trains

A railway is nothing without trains to run on it, so let's look at the Bakerloo's trains.

Original 1906 Gate Stock

The early tubes had mostly followed main-line practice and used locomotives to haul unpowered carriages, with all the attendant problems of getting the loco from one end to the other at termini, though the Waterloo & City Railway had motor cars with driving cabs at each end of the train. In these, the entire traction current went through the driver's controller (which was suitably massive) and along cables on the top of the train. Apart from the safety issues, this made uncoupling a major operation. But by the time that the trains for the Yerkes tubes were being planned, a third alternative was available: motor cars with multiple-unit control. In this, the controller uses low-power circuits, which then operate relays that control the actual traction power. The power can, therefore, be picked up separately by each motor car and there is no need for high-voltage links between vehicles, just small cables that can be safely plugged and unplugged by railway staff. Multiple-unit control was invented by Frank Julian Sprague, a former US naval officer, and was first tried out in 1897 on one of the Chicago 'El' lines. Though this was not one of Yerkes's companies, he no doubt knew what it was doing and

multiple-unit control was first used in London when he took over and electrified the District Line.

Unlike some of the early tube lines, the Bakerloo had the advantage of being part of a group run by people (some from the District, others imported by Yerkes) who had experience of running urban

Frank Sprague; date unknown, but believed to be around the time he invented multiple-unit control. COURTESY JOHN SPRAGUE

Original 1906 Gate Stock motor car number 1. LURS COLLECTION
CDWF03

train services. As a part of this, they put together a consistent design (though with some minor variations) for all three of their tube lines (Bakerloo, Hampstead and Piccadilly), even though there were no physical connections to allow trains to move between them. The first order of these was for the Bakerloo and consisted of thirty-six motor cars (the Yerkes group tended to use US terminology, such as 'car' for 'carriage' and 'truck' for 'bogie', and this has continued into Underground practice), thirty-six trailer cars and thirty-six control trailers. Each car was steel-bodied and 50ft 2¾in (15.310m) long, 8ft 8in or 8ft 11in (2.642 or 2.718m) wide (most sources give the former figure, but Piers Connor suggests, in an article in 2014, reasons to suspect the wider number for at least the initial batch) and 9ft 5⅜in (2.880m) high from rail level to roof, with the floor 22in (56cm) above rail level. The seating in each car consisted of longitudinal seats at each end and traverse pairs in the middle; motor cars had four, twenty-four and eighteen seats in each section, while the others had eighteen, sixteen and eighteen. At the driving end of the motor car the longitudinal seats were three steps up from the remainder and were next to a bulkhead with a door, behind which was the control equipment and then the driving cab. The press described the interiors as 'lavishly decorated', which might have been true relative to horse buses, even though the seats were simply covered with rattan (cane). The outsides were painted in

scarlet up to the bottom of the windows and cream above that point.

The motor cars had two British Thomson-Houston motors rated at 200hp (150kW), both on the same bogie. The control equipment, as was standard at the time, was based on contactors – essentially relays with special features to prevent damage from arcing when the circuit was opened. The space for the control equipment turned out to be too small and, on the other lines, the four raised seats were removed to allow it to be expanded. The end that didn't have the driving cab, and both ends on the trailer cars, had an open platform with a door into the passenger compartment and metal lattice gates across either side; passengers would board and alight through these gates (since all stations on the Bakerloo were underground, this was not a hardship in bad weather). Each pair of adjacent platforms, and the platform at the end of the train if it wasn't a motor car, was managed by a single 'gateman' who opened and closed both the gates and the compartment doors and would ride on the platforms between stations. In the case of a control trailer, one end had driving controls mounted on the platform with a screen to keep the breeze off the driver and a window for him to look through (the idea of seats for drivers was a long way in the future). Each platform had a control for a bell on the platform or driving cab at the other end.

During the Parliamentary process, Yerkes had stated that he would buy British whenever possible. However, it seems that 'possible' was a bit of a movable feast: the Bakerloo rolling stock was ordered from the American Car & Foundry Co. of Berwick, Pennsylvania, who built them and then broke them into convenient pieces for shipping to Manchester, where they were reassembled. The same happened with the Hampstead line's stock, though these were described by the *Railway Times* as being made this time 'almost entirely of British material', while the Piccadilly's trains came from France and Austria-Hungary. (These latter were built in Győr and are normally known as the 'Hungarian Stock'.) Made up into sets of six or twelve cars, they were hauled by a steam locomotive to the LNWR's Camden depot on Saturday nights, starting in September 1905. On arrival there, they were lifted off their bogies and placed on trolleys that could be hauled, one each night, by teams of fourteen horses to London Road depot, where they were reunited with their wheels; since the last trams of the night were at about 02:00, they would have to wait at St George's Circus until then before blocking London Road as they were turned into the depot. One time that the horses were replaced by a traction engine, it broke down at this point and blocked the trams for most of the next day. The London County Council, which operated the trams, was not amused, and no doubt nor were Yerkes's accountants when they got the compensation claim.

The initial service was run with a mixture of three-car and six-car trains, with the longer ones used in peak hours. A three-car train consisted of one vehicle of each type, while a six-car train was two three-car trains with their control trailers coupled together. Obviously, with no way to turn the trains round, each motor car and control trailer was 'handed' or 'ended' and almost certainly there were an equal number that faced in each direction. Each train required a driver and a guard (or 'conductor', as they were called for many years), who stood on the platforms at the rear end of the car being used to drive the train, plus one or four junior gatemen who occupied the remaining positions. When a train was ready to depart, everyone would close their gates and the rear gateman would ring his bell to indicate he had done so and his position was safe to proceed. The next gateman along the train would hear the bell and, when his position was also safe, ring his bell. Eventually this process would reach the guard, whose bell told the driver to start. Thus someone standing on the platform would hear a – hopefully rapid – peal of chimes running along each train.

The original 1906 Stock was in use until it was withdrawn in 1929; the last train actually departed Elephant & Castle for Queen's Park at 00:15 on 1 January 1930.

1914 Stock

While two of the three Yerkes tubes remained essentially unchanged for many years, the Bakerloo had grown longer by nearly 30 per cent by 1913, with more to come, and the initial 108 cars were feeling the strain. It was therefore decided to purchase extra rolling stock. The order consisted of ten motor cars from Brush Electrical Engineering Co. of Loughborough and two motor cars and two trailers from Leeds Forge Co., British manufacturers now being acceptable, it seems. The reason for buying mostly motor cars was that the Piccadilly turned out to have a surplus of control trailer cars from its original 1906 order and ten of these therefore had the control equipment removed and were transferred across; the result was six four-car trains.

The fourteen 1914 vehicles were broadly similar to the 1906 Stock, but with some exceptions. First, they were fitted with electric tail lamps and emergency battery-powered lighting. Up until then, if the power was cut off the passengers got to sit in the dark. But far more noticeable was the extra door in the middle of each car. These doors opened inwards and were sprung so that they closed when not being pushed or held open. Opening and closing the gates on the end platform operated a bolt that locked the door; a green light informed the gateman that the centre doors were closed and bolted and, therefore, it was safe to ring his bell. Inside the trains, the seats were covered with moquette velvet rather than rattan and the Brush cars had armrests. The clerestory roofs of the 1906 Stock were also replaced by a higher arched roof so as to make room for the doors.

1914 Stock motor car 48, one of ten from Brush. LENS OF SUTTON

The motors were more powerful (240hp or 180kW) than the 1906 Stock and they also introduced the 'control governor', which cuts power to the motors if there is insufficient pressure in the brake pipe. The 1914 Stock was scrapped at the same time as the 1906 Stock. (Some websites claim that they lasted until 1935, but the author has been unable to find any evidence to support this claim.)

Borrowed Trains

New trains had been planned for the joint LNWR/ LER service to Watford Junction, but the war meant that these could not be supplied in time for the 1917 opening. Therefore the Bakerloo borrowed ten trailers and ten Hungarian motor cars from the Piccadilly Line – seven of these had been converted from trailers by the LER and had had central doors added like those in the 1914 stock – to make up five more four-car trains for the service to Queen's Park and Willesden Junction. Another seven trailers and nine motor cars were added in 1917.

For the service to Watford Junction, a more radical approach was needed: twenty-two Brush motor cars that had been intended for a delayed Central Line extension (it eventually opened in 1920) were diverted to the Bakerloo and another thirty trailers came from the Piccadilly. These were made up into five-car formations, though some evening peak services were extended to six cars, with the rear one locked out of use until Piccadilly Circus. These trains had problems because of the higher platforms on the shared section. On the Gate Stock trailers it was possible to add a ramp and step totalling 4½in (11.5cm), but the motor cars were completely enclosed, with one central and one end door, and this made that approach impractical; passengers were left to step up some 10in (25cm) to reach the platform. There was also the technical problem that the Central Line had a central positive rail and no negative, so new pick-up shoes had to be added on the outside of the borrowed motor cars. This was possible at the driving cab end, but there was insufficient room at the other end, so the shoes were added to the adjacent trailer car with connecting jump leads.

The borrowed Central Line cars and the last thirty trailers were returned in 1920. The original powered bogies of the motor cars had not withstood the hammering they got from the higher speeds in the open so had had to be replaced by an improved design from Cammell Laird during 1919; Gate Stock motor cars stood in for them.

'Hungarian' Gate Stock of the type borrowed for the Queen's Park extension. LURS COLLECTION 00964

A train believed to be the 1917-20 borrowed stock at Watford Junction. REAL PHOTOGRAPHS/LURS COLLECTION 06823

Watford Joint Stock

In 1914, the LNWR and LER had put in a joint order to the Metropolitan Carriage, Wagon and Finance Co. for seventy-two new cars: thirty-six motor cars; twelve control trailers; and twenty-four trailers. These would be owned two-thirds by the LNWR and one-third by the LER. However, the outbreak of war meant that the factory was diverted to making military vehicles and aircraft, eventually becoming the dominant producer of tanks, and the trains only started to arrive in March 1920, with deliveries taking about a year in total.

The trains were designed specifically for the Watford service. They were completely enclosed with no exterior platform and were much heavier than previous trains in order to reduce vibration. The floors were higher, at 2ft 4in (71cm) above rail level, so as to reduce the step up to platforms on the joint section. The seats (thirty-six in motor cars and forty-eight in trailers) were mostly transverse

and were more comfortable for the longer journeys and the cars were fitted with electric heaters for the winter. Finally, little parcel and hat racks were placed above the windows, the only time this feature appeared on tube trains. The interiors were a soothing cream and white, while the exteriors were the LNWR's standard colour scheme of chocolate below the windows and white from there up.

The trains were marshalled in two parts. For off-peak running, four-car trains consisted of two trailers between two motor cars. During the peaks, a further two cars were added – a control trailer next to the four-car part and a third motor car on the end. The motor cars had a passageway through the electrical compartment so that passengers could escape from either end of the train in an emergency (as with the 1906 Stock and 1914 Stock, the driving cabs had a window on each side with a door in the middle). Cars had swing doors at the end and in the centre; the end doors were worked manually by the 'gateman' (still called this though there were no longer any gates) and the centre ones electrically. Apparently there were problems with the latter, resulting in some nasty accidents. Although the LNWR (and then LMSR) was the majority owner and the trains were sometimes stored at Croxley Green depot, the LER was responsible for their maintenance.

A result of the delivery of the new stock was that the Bakerloo was over-supplied with trains. A number of cars went to the Hampstead line, though eight motor cars ended up back on the Piccadilly Line.

The Joint Stock, with its several gatemen on each train, was costly to run and slow to handle station stops, but all attempts to modernize the door systems failed. So it was withdrawn in 1931; most was scrapped but six motors, two trailers and one control trailer were rebuilt by the LMSR and assembled into three trains to run the Croxley Green and Rickmansworth branch services (the latter had been electrified in 1927), except on Saturdays, when the line was deemed too busy for them to cope. Rickmansworth station staff particularly disliked them because it was much harder to load skips of watercress (a major local product)

ACTON WORKS

Until 1922, all maintenance and repairs of trains was done at individual line depots. But once money became available after World War I, the LER looked at building a single depot that could handle all major work, leaving the line depots to do cleaning, minor repairs and general maintenance. The site chosen was on former market gardens on the south side of the District Line just east of Acton Town station. This handled all major overhauls, first for LER trains and, after the formation of the LPTB, for all Underground trains.

Initially, major overhauls for motor cars were at 50,000-mile (80,000km) intervals, meaning approximately yearly, with trailers allowed to run about 40 per cent further. Over time, as equipment got more reliable and some requirements (such as rewinding motor coils) went away, this period extended until it had reached nine years. In 1985, with much of Acton's own equipment needing replacement, it was decided to move maintenance back to the lines.

Acton Works remains to carry out specialist work like overhauling equipment after it has been removed from trains and tenders for various projects; for example, it converted the Metropolitan's A60 Stock to one-person operation. It will take over most of the work currently being done at Lillie Bridge Depot when that closes.

---

through the narrow doorways into the luggage compartments. The trains had a headlight under each of the windows at the front and, so that signalmen could distinguish them, those on the Croxley Green branch would have the left (as seen from the front) lit, while the right-hand lamp was used for the Rickmansworth branch. It is believed that both lamps together were used to indicate an empty train running between Watford Junction and Croxley Green depot. The ex-Joint Stock trains were withdrawn from these branches on the outbreak of World War II and scrapped in 1949.

1920 Stock

In 1920, Cammell Laird had built twenty trailers and twenty control trailers to allow Piccadilly Line trains to be lengthened to six cars. These were the first tube trains to be built with the air-powered sliding doors ('air doors' for short) that we are now used to. There were two double-leaf doors – each with a central pillar – along the length of each side, plus a single-leaf door at each corner. Unlike previous stock, all forty-four seats were longitudinal with no armrests; standing passengers were given poles to grab on to. Scarily for modern times, the floors were asbestos cement. The first few cars had sensitive rubber edges on the doors, causing them to reopen if blocked, but the operational disadvantages of this were soon realized. Little yellow arms stuck out of the side of the car if any of the doors were open; the guards (now only one at each end, since there were no manual gates to operate) were supposed to check that they had all retreated into the car body before ringing the departure bell. However, the arms turned out to be another mistake, being prone to breaking off. The rest of the production run was instead fitted with what is now standard: a door interlock circuit (also known as the traction interlock), which runs through every door engine and requires them all to be closed before the driver can apply power or even – on modern trains – release the brakes.

By the late 1920s the Piccadilly had extensions in the open air in the planning stage, for which the

1920 Stock cars would be unsuitable because they didn't cope with the rain. Therefore, they were replaced by Standard Stock and then rebuilt internally to have forty-eight seats (some traverse), armrests and wooden flooring. They were then combined with twenty Standard Stock motor cars to provide the Bakerloo with trains that ran (though only as far north as Queen's Park) from 1932 until 1938, when they were mostly scrapped.

Standard Stock

The Cammell Laird trailers showed the direction in which tube train design should go, while at the same time the LER found itself needing much new stock because of the major changes about to happen on what would become the Northern Line. It was also clear that, despite teething troubles, air doors at intervals along the car were far superior to Gate Stock. The LER therefore decided to have built what became known as the Standard Stock.

In 1922, five companies were each asked to build a trailer car to the same basic specification: forty-eight seats and two double-leaf doors on each side within a standard set of dimensions. The LER's own staff also designed a control trailer to the same specification. The manufacturers were clearly trying to impress and gain the business: one car even had glass lampshades that would hardly survive rush-hour crowding. The LER's own design was chosen and an initial order of 191 cars was shared between three of the companies (not including the glass lampshade one!). Eventually 1,460 cars (645 motors, 546 trailers and 269 control trailers) were built in 18 batches between 1923 and 1934.

The Standard Stock was clearly the way of the future: a single guard could now handle four cars and, once intercoms were added to trains, even a seven-car train, greatly reducing the wage bill, even though a guard on air-door trains was paid an extra 4s 10d per week. The air doors also easily halved the time that a train stopped at a station; between Elephant & Castle and Queen's Park this could represent a saving of six minutes, meaning, for example, that a 15tph service could be increased to 18tph with the same number of trains. In 1929, the Bakerloo's Gate Stock was replaced by Union Construction Co. Standard Stock (also known as 'Felthams' after the location of the factory).

Much of the Standard Stock left the Bakerloo in 1938. What Standard Stock was left was marshalled into seven-car formations, with two motor cars at the north end and one at the south. These were restricted to the Stanmore branch once it joined the Bakerloo, because the trains' lower speed compared with the new 1938 Stock was less important there. However, the mixture of trains turned into an operational nightmare – fast trains were catching up with slow ones on the central section, destroying the even spacing needed for efficient operation in rush hour – and twelve of the seventeen Standard Stock trains were replaced during the war by 1938 Stock not needed on the Northern Line because of wartime delays to extension work there. In 1946, delayed work to extend platforms on the Watford branch was completed and fifty-eight Standard Stock trailers built in 1927 were converted to work with the 1938 Stock so that the latter could be lengthened to seven cars. The converted trailers were known internally as '58' trailers.

Table 3 Standard Stock Manufacturers

Birmingham Railway Carriage & Wagon Co.*	175	
Cammell Laird & Co. Ltd*	154	
Metropolitan Carriage, Wagon & Finance Co.*	617	
Metropolitan-Cammell Carriage & Wagon Co. Ltd	233	Formed by a merger of the previous two in 1929
Gloucester Railway Carriage & Wagon Co.*	40	1931 batch only
Union Construction Company	241	A dormant UERL company reactivated in 1927

* These four, plus the Leeds Forge Company, built the demonstration trailers; the Gloucester company also built the LER's design.

Watford Joint Stock motor car 23J at London Road in 1920. HMRS

'Watford Replacement Stock' was the name given to a 1930 order of sixty-two cars of Standard Stock that formed a direct replacement for the Watford Joint Stock. Because of the longer and faster runs on the surface they were fitted with electro-pneumatic (EP) brakes, which were faster-acting than the traditional ones, plus a 'weak-field' circuit, which, once the motors had reached their normal maximum speed, reduced the back elec-tromotive force that imposed that limit and thus allowed them to run even faster at the cost of higher current consumption. To prevent it wasting power on the congested tube sections, a 'flag switch' was soon added, which enabled or disabled the use of weak field. The switch was (and is, on those trains still fitted with DC motors) a plate mounted behind the right-hand front window that swings forward from horizontal (off) to vertical (on). The top of

Standard Stock train to Watford on the New Lines, believed to be at Wembley Central.
LURS COLLECTION 01429

A southbound train of Watford Replacement Stock departs Kenton in 1937, seen shortly before it passes under the Metropolitan Line. The blue stripe at window level tells passengers at central London stations that this train goes north of Queen's Park. COLOUR-RAIL.COM

the plate is striped black and yellow, letting staff outside the train see if weak field has been turned on where it shouldn't be. Both EP braking and weak field were eventually added to all Standard Stock motor cars.

The 'Bakerloo Harrow cars' were a set of forty-two Feltham cars built in 1928 and fitted with EP braking and weak field in 1932 to allow them to move to the Bakerloo. Two more 1928 and four 1929 Felthams were poached from the Piccadilly, which had already modified them. The eight resulting trains allowed a 4tph service between Elephant & Castle and Harrow & Wealdstone to be added.

Apart from the 58 trailers, the last Standard Stock trains ran on the Bakerloo Line on 23 May 1949, after which they were moved to other lines.

1938 Stock and 1949 Stock

Technology moves on, and by the mid-1930s it was possible to put all of the motor and control equipment for a tube train underneath the floor. The Underground loved this idea: until then, 20 per cent

of the space in a motor car was occupied by equipment instead of paying passengers. An experimental batch of twenty-four cars was built and given the name '1935 Stock'. While technically advanced, they fell foul of someone who had seen the *Fliegender Hamburger* and decided that what tube lines needed was a streamlined train with a semicircular cab that used up much of the space saved by eliminating the equipment compartment and looked ridiculous when two cab ends were coupled together. Thankfully this brainstorm was restricted to eighteen of these cars and the Bakerloo never saw them. In 1952, these cars were rebuilt as (flat-ended) trailers and merged into the 1938 Stock fleet.

Within a year of the 1935 Stock coming into service the LPTB issued an order for 750 new cars, later increased to 1,121; 370 were built by the Birmingham Railway Carriage & Wagon Co. and the rest by Metropolitan-Cammell. These were the 1938 Stock.

As well as the obvious difference of the equipment being under the floor, these cars had more subtle changes. The low-voltage power for lighting

1938 Stock southbound at Stonebridge Park. LURS COLLECTION 04122

and for the control equipment was no longer derived directly from the current rails, but rather from a motor-generator, meaning that the lights did not go out when the train went over point-work. Standing passengers were assisted by rubber handgrips hanging from the ceiling. The electro-pneumatic brakes were controlled via a mercury switch that automatically reduced the braking pressure as the train slowed so as to stop the brakes locking up. There were two stages of weak field and the power system used nine notches, with resistors being switched in and out of circuit as a camshaft rotated and the motor circuitry switched from series to series–parallel to parallel, the whole process being automatic with the driver merely selecting 'wet rails' or 'dry rails' for the acceleration rate.

The cars were assembled into semi-permanent sets through bar couplings and forty-core cables. At the outer end of each set, the motor car had a 'Wedgelock' coupler beneath the driving cab. When two of these were driven (carefully) together and a button pressed in one cab, the coupler automatically made a physical lock between the cars and also made all the necessary electrical and pneumatic connections – in the right order – to allow the two units to operate as one. It is still the standard coupler used on the Underground.

The 1938 Stock added a fourth kind of car: the non-driving motor (NDM), which was a motor car with no driving cab, controlled remotely from another (driving) motor. The trains were intended to be assembled into three-car units – with two motor cars and one trailer – and four-car units – with an NDM as well. One of each would then be coupled to form a seven-car train. There were two variants of driving car: the 'A' car with a solid centre buffer above the coupler and the 'D' car with a spring-loaded buffer. The 'A' cars were kept at the north end of Bakerloo trains and care had to be taken not to turn them round during a visit to Croxley Green depot.

1938 and 1972 Stock at Neasden sidings. LURS COLLECTION 00431

'D'?

Why is it 'D' and not 'B'? The reason is that the four axles of each car are labelled from A to D in order. Therefore each car has an 'A' end and a 'D' end; this nomenclature then carries over to the complete train. Only some types of rolling stock care about this, while others are agnostic and there is no problem on lines like the Victoria or the post-Croxley Bakerloo where there is no way to reverse a train.

The cars were 51ft 2¾in (15.615m) long (except the driving motor cars, which were 13in [330mm] longer), 8ft 6³⁄₁₆in (2.595m) wide and 9ft 5½in (2.883m) high from rail level. Each car had forty-four seats, two sets of double-leaf doors on each side and single-leaf doors at each corner, all air-worked except for those in the driving cabs. The window beside each door was double-glazed, with the door sliding into the gap between the panes. The doors were fitted with passenger controls and opened much faster as a result of the redesign necessary to have doors on the same side not all working together. There were sixteen traverse seats in the middle and a tip-up seat in the end wall at each corner passenger door; the remainder were longitudinal. The motors were only rated at 122hp (91kW) continuous or 168hp (125kW) for one hour, less than those on Standard Stock, which was one reason for the extra motor cars.

1938 Stock started to arrive on the Bakerloo on 2 January 1939 and, by the start of the next year, all twenty-five trains used on the Watford branch and three of the twenty used on the Stanmore branch were 1938 Stock. However, as described earlier, these were initially only six cars long.

During World War II, the 1938 Stock was involved in a mystery. Staff found that the rubber hand grips hanging from the roof – provided for standing passengers to support themselves – were disappearing, leaving only the connecting spring behind. It became clear that these were being used as impromptu coshes, but LT did not want to admit it. However, when one turned up in Algiers they were able to advertise that Commandos were using them as weapons and it was all in aid of the war effort. The hand grips were redesigned in 1943 to be impractical to detach.

To cool down passengers in hot weather, one Bakerloo Line car was fitted with four fans in 1947; these sucked air into the roof space and then circulated it back round through side vents. This car was later moved to the Northern Line and the fans were removed in 1952.

There were not enough 1938 Stock trains after the war and in 1948 the LTE decided to buy eighty-nine new cars and modify thirty-eight others. A month later, the Bakerloo extension to Camberwell

*Inside a 1938 Stock motor car
after the Jubilee Line opened.
LURS COLLECTION CDWF04*

was announced, messing up the numbers. Further changes in plans took place until, in June 1950, the LTE settled on twenty new trailers and seventy uncoupling non-driving motors (UNDM). These latter were motor cars but with the cab and controls removed, replaced by simplified shunting controls in a cabinet. This new 1949 Stock was otherwise very similar to the 1938 Stock – the major visible difference was the lack of tip-up seats – and they were absorbed into the 1938 Stock fleet once they started arriving in November 1951. Twenty-two existing NDMs were also converted into UNDMs at the same time. By the time the dust settled, or so people thought, the Bakerloo had fifty-four seven-car trains all with '58' trailers in the three-car portion (four of the trains had '58s' in both portions); thirty-one of these trains also had UNDMs in the three-car portion.

However, the new UNDMs were to cause unexpected trouble. On 5 June 1950, the Bakerloo reintroduced uncoupling, with some trains reduced from seven to four cars off-peak and the three-car portion parked in a siding or depot. This was fine in most circumstances, but sometimes it meant

driving a unit from Watford Junction to Croxley Green depot – a distance of about 1½ miles (2.4km) – using only the rudimentary controls of the UNDM with no 'deadman' and only a small window in the connecting door to look through. Drivers did not like this and made it clear; in the end, about half of the portions containing UNDMs were swapped with the Piccadilly for ones with cabs at both ends, while the remainder were carefully scheduled not to uncouple at Watford.

In 1949, a Bakerloo driving motor, number 10306 (recall that the Bakerloo opened on 10 March 1906), was modified to test some new ideas for future stock. One idea involved extending the windows, both in the doors and the body, up into the curved roof to allow standing passengers to see the names of stations. To prevent the body flexing too much, the windows next to the doors were replaced by small round ones. The extended door windows were a feature of all future stock from 1967 onwards, but, even though they made the interior feel more spacious, the large fixed windows let in too much heat in summer and were abandoned, allowing the portholes to revert to rectangles.

A 1938 Stock train runs into the
shed at Queen's Park to reverse on
20 November 1985, the final day
of passenger service of this stock.
LURS COLLECTION 85XA5

Car 10306 with the experimental windows at Acton Works. *R.J. GREENAWAY/LURS COLLECTION 02169*

Passenger door control, though fitted from new, was only brought into use on the Bakerloo on 19 December 1949 and was taken out of use again in March 1959. While passengers liked it, particularly in cold weather on the outside sections, it was technically troublesome. The final straw was when it was discovered that, on modified Standard Stock, disabling the passenger door controls in some situations also disabled several safety devices!

During the 1970s, thirty-six of the remaining 1938 Stock trains on the Bakerloo underwent an Extra Heavy Overhaul to allow them to last an extra ten years and by the end of 1977 these were the only ones left on the line. Two were removed following service reductions in November 1981 and eighteen went over the next two years. The last 1938 Stock train on the Bakerloo was the 18:52 from Elephant & Castle to Stonebridge Park on 20 November 1985.

1959 Stock

The 1959 Stock consisted of seventy-six seven-car trains built for the Piccadilly Line and arriving there

---

STARLIGHT EXPRESS

The last 1938 Stock working was carried out by a train in a special livery sponsored by a theatre agency; as a result it was commonly known as the 'Starlight Express'. After this final service it was retained for enthusiasts' tours, then, from 1986 to 1988 it acquired an 'as worn in 1938' livery and operated on the Northern Line. The motor cars from the three-car portion now form train 483007 on the Isle of Wight's Island Line, while the trailer from that portion and the NDM from the four-car portion were scrapped. The remainder of the four-car portion is preserved at the London Transport Museum Depot in Acton. It is expected that 483007 will be replaced by a class 484 train – itself rebuilt from two cars of a District Line D78 train – in 2020.

---

between 1959 and 1964, fifty-seven of them having spent time as eight-car trains on the Central Line. The main innovations compared with 1938 Stock were unpainted aluminium alloy bodies instead of painted steel, fluorescent lighting and automatic couplers. The traction motors were 80hp (60kW) continuous rating – the lighter bodies reduced the power requirements and the maximum current that the substations needed to provide.

1959 Stock motor cars 1044 and 1045 in retirement on Alderney. ROBIN OAKLEY

However, the 1959 Stock did not spend much time on the Bakerloo. It first arrived in 1983 when fifteen trains were freed up by service reductions on other lines. In 1985, the arrival of 1983 Stock on the Jubilee Line allowed its 1972 Mark II Stock (itself originally from the Bakerloo) to move to the Northern Line, allowing it to in turn cascade another sixteen trains of 1959 Stock to finally replace the 1938 Stock. The following year, thirteen of these went back, swapped for 1972 Mark II Stock, followed by the remainder in the next three years. Two of the motor cars that ran on the Bakerloo are now to be found on Alderney.

1972 Mark II Stock

When the GLC took over London Transport in 1970, it discovered that the rolling stock situation was in a mess, partly because the 1938 Stock was wearing out and partly because industrial action at Acton Works was preventing parts from being repaired. After a senior politician travelled on the Northern Line during rush hour, he kicked the LTE into Doing Something. Some calculations showed that,

although the line would get seventy-nine trains of 1959 Stock from the Piccadilly when the new trains for the Heathrow extension arrived, that still left it thirty trains short. These would have to be bought new.

Rather than wasting time coming up with a brand-new design, the 1972 Stock was a variation of the 1967 Stock designed for the Victoria Line, reduced from eight cars to seven per train. The four-car portion has two driving motors and two trailers; the three-car portion has an UNDM at one end. Both ends of the four-car portion and the UNDM have automatic couplers, but the remaining driving motor has a mechanical coupler, since – it was hoped – it would only ever couple to a train in distress. Each motor bogie has two 80hp (60kW) motors wired permanently in series. The cars are 52ft 5in (15.98m) long (driving motors are 4in [10cm] longer), 8ft 8in (2.64m) wide and 9ft 5¼in (2.88m) high, with the normal arrangement of doors except that the driving cab is doorless – the driver must enter and exit from the passenger compartment or the emergency end door. Obviously they had traditional controls rather than being set

1972 Mark II Stock in its original colour scheme at Canons Park; the ornate lamps are long gone.
LURS COLLECTION 01438

up for automatic operation. There are forty seats in the motored cars and thirty-six in the trailers.

In 1971, a second batch of thirty-three trains was ordered in order to keep Metro-Cammell (the builder) from collapsing; nominally these were for the first stage of the Fleet Line. The main difference from the first batch was that they had provision for automatic working included, justifying the division into Mark I and Mark II; this made them slightly lighter. Visually they were also different, as the Mark IIs had red doors and a bold red circle-and-bar on the otherwise unpainted aluminium body. On the Bakerloo, the A end of the four-car unit is at the south end and the D end of the three-car at the north end (the opposite of 1938 Stock).

Though they were initially delivered to the Northern Line during 1973–4, in early 1977 they started to be moved to the Bakerloo and entered service on 4 April. After some technical modifications the first one reached Watford Junction on 14 October. By the following month there were seventeen on the Bakerloo; another six arrived next year and the last ten in 1979, ready for the opening of the Jubilee Line. On 30 April, all the 1972 Stock trains berthed on the Stanmore branch and the 1938 Stock trains on the Watford branch and the central section, so that the next day the two fleets were ready to run on their separate lines.

As already described, all thirty-three trains of the 1972 Mark II Stock returned to the Bakerloo in the late 1980s. Between 1990 and 1995, all underwent extensive renovation to meet recommendations following the King's Cross fire in 1987 and reappeared in a new livery of off-white body, blue 'skirt', and red doors and ends. This colour scheme was created by an engineer at Acton Works, Mark Orsman, who was inspired by liveries on suburban trains in the Paris area. Four Mark I trains (minus two cars) were also upgraded to be compatible with the Mark II and assigned to the Bakerloo as well. They underwent further refurbishment between 2014 and 2019. There are now thirty-six trains on the Bakerloo, the oldest rolling stock on any urban transit system in the UK.

Marker Light codes

The Standard, 1938 and 1949 Stock had marker lights beneath the left (as seen from the front) window. These were lit in different patterns to inform other staff – particularly signallers – which train this was. It is not clear when these codes came into use on the various stocks, but they died out around 1962, after which the bottom right lamp became a red tail lamp.

Inside 1972 Stock 'D end' driving motor 3552 at the front of a service departing Elephant & Castle in June 2019. The door at the end is the driver's normal route into the cab.

Standard Stock marker light codes.

Service to Watford Junction
Service from Watford Junction
From Croxley Green depot

Empty to Watford Junction
To Croxley Green depot

Service to and from Harrow & Wealdstone

1938 Stock marker light codes.

Watford Junction

Harrow & Wealdstone

Harrow & Wealdstone
(empty)

Queen's Park

London Road depot

Elephant & Castle

Stanmore

Wembley Park

Neasden

Watford Junction (empty)
Croxley Green depot

CHAPTER 13

Signalling

Trains need a long distance in which to stop, so can't be driven 'on sight' like cars. That makes the signalling an important part of the railway. As with rolling stock, being part of the Yerkes group meant that the Bakerloo was not using trial and error, but, rather, was being run by people with experience.

The system used was the same as Westinghouse had installed on the District Line in 1905 and which, in turn, was derived from an installation on the Boston Elevated Railway. The line is track-circuited throughout and these are used to control the signals. On plain track, the signals clear automatically once the relevant track circuits are unoccupied, while where there is pointwork a signalman controls the signals, *but* they still won't clear until the correct track circuits are unoccupied, even though the operating lever has been pulled. The Westinghouse signals consisted of an oil lamp that was covered by a metal plate containing two pieces of coloured glass; pneumatic pressure moved the plate up to show green or down to show red. (Over the years the oil lamps, which tended to be blown out by moving trains, were replaced by electric ones and eventually the moving plate was replaced by separate lamps.)

Each signal was also fitted with a train stop: a small lever beside the track that was lowered by pneumatic pressure when the signal was green

and raised by a spring when it was red. In the latter situation, it was high enough to catch a matching tripcock lever on the train, which caused the brakes to be applied automatically and stop the train. An overlap track circuit of 400ft (120m) was provided after each signal, giving room for the train to stop after being 'tripped'; a signal cannot clear while the next signal's overlap is occupied. Today, the length of the overlap is computed based on the maximum speed and the gradient, but the principle remains the same.

Each signal box had a frame of miniature levers to work the points and signals. These were, of course, fully interlocked so that a signal lever could not be pulled unless the relevant points were in the right position and pulling it locked the points in that position (this had become a legal requirement in 1889). In addition, they each had an illuminated diagram – a novelty at the time – that showed the position of the points and the status of each track circuit. This had the layout painted on glass with lamps behind it for each track circuit. When the track circuit was occupied, the lamps went out and the section of track turned black.

Initially, there were three signal boxes, at London Road, Lambeth North and Marylebone; one was added at Elephant & Castle when it opened. When trains started reversing at Edgware Road it gained its own signal box and the Marylebone one

Inside Queen's Park (Bakerloo) signal box, showing the levers and illuminated diagram.
GRAHAM FLOYD

TRACK CIRCUITS

Track circuits are the basis of modern signalling. In the simplest case – the DC track circuit initially used on the Bakerloo – the track is divided into sections by pieces of insulating material in the join between two lengths of rail. A battery or other supply is connected to the two rails at one end of the section and a relay detects it at the other. A train is a big piece of metal short-circuiting this, meaning the relay drops out, indicating that the track is occupied. The same happens if any of the wires break or the battery goes flat, making the system 'fail-safe'.

Insulated block joint.

was moved from above the crossover to the south-bound platform. The London Road signal box was initially above the tunnel mouths and had a pneumatically controlled semaphore signal in the open air rather than the coloured lights. Most of the depot points were hand-worked. As the line was extended further, signal boxes were added at Paddington and Queen's Park, the latter also using pneumatic semaphore signals. In 1914, a crossover and signal box were added at Piccadilly Circus, while the next year the London Road box was closed, Lambeth North taking over its duties.

Once a Bakerloo train had run through the shed at the north end of Queen's Park and was on the New Lines, it was subject to the LNWR's traditional semaphore signals controlled by equally traditional mechanical signal boxes. Even though most of the New Lines were beside the four main tracks, they had their own signal boxes rather than the existing

ones being given more jobs. This system managed for many years, but by the end of the 1920s, with the heavy traffic on the New Lines, it was clearly struggling to cope.

At which point it fell into the hands of A.F. Bound.

Bound designed a completely new signalling system for the New Lines. This covered the route from its start at Camden, just outside Euston, all the way to the new platforms at Watford Junction. Signals were generally of the searchlight type, where a single head can show all three colours, and the line was track-circuited throughout. Most of the 201 signals in the system were automatic, while many of those that weren't could still be left to work themselves much of the time. This allowed the line to be run by only eight signal boxes (Camden No.2, Queen's Park No.3, Willesden New Station, Stonebridge Park Power House, Harrow No.2, Colne Junction, Watford High Street and Watford Junction No.4), while nine signal

Harrow No. 2 signal box only handled the New Lines, leaving No. 1 to handle the far busier main lines.
LURS COLLECTION 01728

A.F. BOUND

Arthur Frank Bound was the *enfant terrible* of the British railway signalling world. He started his career on the London, Brighton and South Coast Railway before moving to the British Pneumatic Railway Signal Company. In 1906, he became assistant signal superintendent of the Great Central Railway, rising to the top job. In the early days of the Institution of Railway Signal Engineers (IRSE) he scandalized a meeting by saying that signalling should be so obvious that drivers would not need to learn the route before driving over it.

In February 1915, Bound gave a paper to the IRSE that basically tore apart all the existing notions and complacency about the block system. He suggested that the way of the future was to completely track-circuit lines and let the signals operate themselves on plain lines, allowing block working to be abolished. The coded bells would be replaced by train describers that passed along information about trains as they progressed. Signals should be designed to tell the driver what speed to run at, rather than just when to stop. Three-position signals should therefore be used to give drivers more information about the line ahead. This collection of heresies started a spirited debate that occupied three more meetings and ranged over a large number of topics. It seems, though, that few of his contemporaries were convinced by these novel ideas. Nevertheless, he was respected and in 1922 he chaired an IRSE committee on three-aspect signals that introduced the yellow and double yellow aspects essential to modern rail operations in Britain (which mostly match his original suggestions). In 1925, he spent a year as President of the IRSE.

In 1929, Bound became Chief Signal and Telegraph Engineer of the mighty LMSR. He started introducing track-circuiting and colour-light distant signals *en masse*. In March 1932, he gave another paper to the IRSE, proposing a system of speed signals that used three aspects on each signal; from top to bottom they cleared if the train was taking a fast, medium or slow speed route, while the other two stayed red. Bound essentially wanted the IRSE to agree to scrapping the existing signalling conventions and move UK practice to speed signalling. Later the same year Bound set up an experimental installation of his scheme on the main lines at Mirfield, which lasted until May 1970. It was a simplified version of this scheme that would be installed on the New Lines.

The signal aspects on the New Lines were unique. On most of the route there were stop signals, each with a repeater signal approaching it. In normal circumstances the stop signal either showed two red lights, mounted vertically, or green, while the repeater showed a yellow or a green. However, when there was a train between the repeater and the end of the overlap of the stop signal, the repeater also showed two vertical red lights, but with the lower one offset to the left. Of course, normally a driver would not see this because the previous stop signal would still be at danger. The stop signals had electrically powered train stops, but the repeaters didn't.

However, the system was designed to be robust against track circuit failures, which were deemed to be the greatest risk. If a train came to a halt at a red stop signal then, just over a minute later and provided the overlap was clear, the train stop would lower and the lower red lamp would go out, to be replaced by a small yellow one. This gave the driver permission to proceed as far as the next repeater signal, prepared to stop if another train was on the line. If the repeater was still showing double reds, the driver would wait another minute before proceeding cautiously towards the next signal. While this system was no doubt good at dealing with failures, it could result in several trains lined up nose to tail at a signal. It was also the cause of a couple of collisions, as we shall see in the next chapter.

At junctions there were two signals side by side, one for each route; if one route was deemed more important its signal was slightly higher. If one direction led to a line using traditional signalling, that signal did not have a lower lamp, because the calling-on process was not available. If advance warning of the junction was required, the previous signal would have yellow lamps on either side of it, the *left* lamp lighting when the right-hand route was set at the junction and *vice versa*. In a few cases signals were close enough that one stop signal would also act as a repeater for the next one, showing double red, yellow or green. At least one junction repeater could show a double yellow aspect when the junction signal was yellow,

boxes on plain line were completely closed and four others that only controlled emergency crossovers (South Hampstead, Kilburn, Wembley and Hatch End) were normally left unmanned. When the two power signal boxes opened in 1964 and 1965, respectively, Watford Junction replaced the two Watford boxes and Euston took over Camden's area. Colne Junction was abolished when the curve closed in 1966, while Willesden took over the territories of the boxes on either side in 1977.

Signal HD1 on the northbound at Harlesden shows a double red stop aspect now the train has partly passed it. The A between the heads indicates that this signal works automatically. LURS COLLECTION 01150

Signal WJ134 (formerly HS2/9) at Watford High Street in May 1973. The left head (with small yellow) reads towards Bushey and the right one towards Croxley Green. Note the BR-style shunt signal at the bottom, probably added in 1964 when Watford Junction PSB took over. ADRIAN PUTLEY

Signal WL2 at the end of the southbound platform at Willesden Junction in April 1983. The left head reads towards the North London Line and so has no lower red light. The circle would light up with a message like 'TRACK DEAD'. ADRIAN PUTLEY

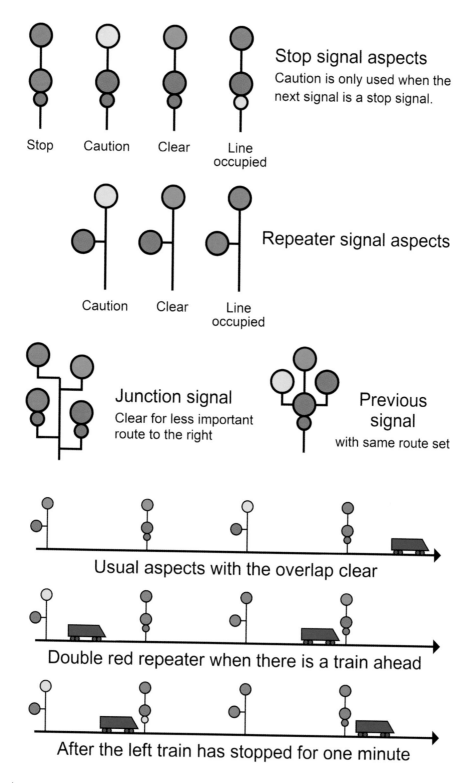

Stop signal aspects
Caution is only used when the next signal is a stop signal.

Stop   Caution   Clear   Line occupied

Repeater signal aspects

Caution   Clear   Line occupied

Junction signal
Clear for less important route to the right

Previous signal
with same route set

Usual aspects with the overlap clear

Double red repeater when there is a train ahead

After the left train has stopped for one minute

New Line signals aspects and typical scenarios.

resulting in a triangle of yellow lights. In later years some of the searchlight signals were replaced by ones with separate lamps for each colour. On the northbound approach to Willesden and Watford Junctions, the small yellow lamp appeared without delay to give permission to enter an occupied platform.

The acquisition of the Stanmore branch resulted in a number of changes to the signalling. As described in Chapter 8, the Metropolitan Line had to be completely rearranged with new signals. Unlike the old main-line style of signalling, with many signals still being semaphores, these were simple red/green stop signals using separate lamps for each colour. When a repeater signal was needed at the same location as a stop signal, it was placed underneath it and only lit up when the stop signal was green. Fog repeaters, mostly of the searchlight type, were also provided on the immediate approach to most stop signals; these could be turned on and off according to the weather (this had also been done in the previous signalling). The new signalling was controlled from six boxes: at Finchley Road (named just 'MD'); Willesden Green ('ME'); either end of Neasden depot ('MF' and 'MH'); Wembley Park ('MG'); and Stanmore ('MK'); all were new except the one at Wembley Park. Baker Street also gained a signal box ('BM') to handle the new junction. The box code appeared as part of the identification of controlled signals.

The rest of the Bakerloo was resignalled to current standards at the same time and gained new lever frames either immediately, or in 1941. These boxes were: 'BB' at Queen's Park; 'BD' at Paddington; 'BP' at Piccadilly Circus; 'BR' at Lambeth North; and 'BS' at Elephant & Castle. The crossover at Lambeth North was also upgraded to a scissors. Additional speed-control signals were added to allow trains to close up at busy stations (these cleared when an approaching train had been proved to reduce its speed sufficiently) and signals (with 'FBX' prefixes) were installed to protect the new floodgates. In addition, a signal was added to allow trains to run northbound on the southbound track from Embankment to Piccadilly Circus if they

A fog repeater warning of a red signal ahead.

were already past the latter when the floodgates closed. One unusual feature of the Piccadilly Circus box was that (until 1980) it also controlled the starting signals on the Piccadilly Line. This allowed the last trains on each line each night – which should all be departing at the same time – to be held until passengers had had a chance to interchange.

More upgrades were done in the post-war years: Queen's Park lost its semaphores in 1953 and in 1955 the Stanmore branch had more signals added to allow trains to run 2 minutes apart instead of 3½.

In 1986, a computer-based control centre was opened for the Metropolitan and Jubilee Lines at Baker Street. This was based around two computers that operated all the signalling under the supervision of a senior signalman, who had a large wall diagram to show what was happening and computer terminals to dig into details and issue instructions. The signal boxes were replaced by Interlocking Machine Rooms (IMR), basically remote-controlled signal boxes that were temporarily operated from control panels in the old boxes before migrating to Baker Street control. A second room was added in April 1988 to allow the Bakerloo Line to work the same way, though the conversion took more than three years. Lambeth North and Elephant & Castle signal boxes were replaced by two IMRs at Waterloo.

By 1988, the New Lines signalling had reached the end of its life and faults were causing delays and possibly at least one collision. It was decided that the calling-on arrangement was no longer necessary and the line was converted to use standard two- and three-aspect signalling. The seventy-six signals (plus three removed when the Croxley Green branch finally closed) are controlled from a computer terminal in Willesden power signal box. Since then, the signalling has remained the same with no change in sight.

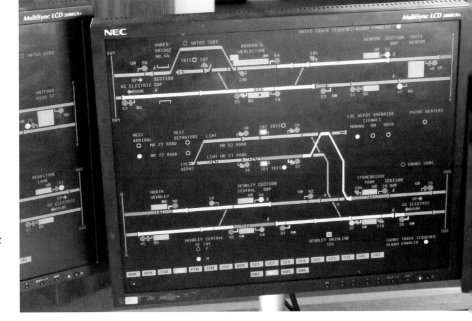

Control screen at Willesden signal box. A northbound Bakerloo train is at Wembley Central and a southbound at Stonebridge Park, with another waiting to come out of the depot.
PETER BENNET

CHAPTER 14

Safety and Danger

Safety

While the primary mechanisms for protecting trains are the signalling and the drivers' vigilance, other features were also added to the Underground in general and the Bakerloo in particular.

The one that everybody knows about is the 'dead man's handle', or 'deadman': the driver needs to press the controller down against a spring and, if they let go for any reason – whether deliberately, accidentally, or because of illness – the traction power is cut off and the brakes applied. This is so obvious that it was fitted from new. In November 1989, the Bakerloo started One Person Operation (OPO), with no guard and the driver operating the doors. This required changes to the deadman, so that it would automatically alert the line controller if it was released for more than a minute; the controller can also talk directly to the train passengers via the train radio described below.

Traditionally, when a train broke down or was delayed while above ground, the driver or guard would walk to the nearest signal box or signal with a telephone and let the signaller know there was an issue. But what about when you're down in a small iron tube? Walking along the track is dangerous: there's an electrified rail on one side and another between the rails. The tunnel is not big enough for a separate walkway. What do you do?

Yerkes's engineers had the answer. Two bare wires were fitted along the side of the tunnel and every driver carried a handset. If they found themselves stuck in a tunnel, the driver would clip the handset to the wires and could then talk to the substation attendant, who would cut off the power if necessary (in the early days the wires connected to the adjacent stations, which then connected the circuit to the substation). Around 1921 the system was modified so that pinching the wires together or clipping a handset to them alerted the relevant substation and, in 1924, this was changed again to cut the power off and turn on the tunnel lights automatically when the wires were pinched together.

However, if the driver needed to talk to the line controller, for example if it was necessary to detrain passengers, the message had to be relayed through the substation attendant, with the risk of misunderstandings. Between 1952 and 1956, the wires gained a second use: a device called DRICO ('DRIver-COntroller'). Clipping a pair of wires fixed in the cab to the tunnel wires allowed the driver to talk directly to the controller using the driver–guard intercom; DRICO did not cut off the power or turn on the lights, but the previous mechanisms still worked.

DRICO had issues: the controller can't call a train that has not been clipped to the wires and, obviously, it can't be used on the move. In

Tunnel telephone wires (Wood Lane closed station, Central Line).

November 1972, the Bakerloo tunnels between Elephant & Castle and Finchley Road were fitted with 'leaky feeder' cables (co-axial cables with holes in the mesh shield to allow radio waves out), while radio masts were erected on the surface part of the Stanmore branch every 2 miles (3km) or so. Four 1938 Stock trains had radios fitted with aerials on the outside of the cab. The drivers and controllers could now talk directly by radio both when stationary and on the move. On 8 August 1977, the experimental system was replaced by a permanent

one covering the entire line (and the Jubilee Line two years later) and its rolling stock. DRICO was retired from the Bakerloo, though it remained on the other lines until 1992 as they waited their turn to be fitted.

Once the Bakerloo was extended to Watford, there was a risk that a full-size LNWR train would be signalled into the Bakerloo platforms at Queen's Park and thence down the tunnels, smashing into the tunnel portal. Curiously, nobody seemed to have been concerned about this, possibly because

Start of the descent from Queen's Park into the Bakerloo tunnels. The 'D OFF' sign reminds drivers to turn off the de-icing equipment. GRAHAM FLOYD

U tubes at Finchley Road station, hanging from the gantry at the right.
RICHARD VINCE

it would require two signalmen (LNWR and LER) and a driver to all make the same mistake. Even after the 1932 resignalling of the New Lines, there were still two signal boxes involved, though Rule 85 for the lines read 'In no circumstances must a L.M.S. train be allowed to run on to the L.P.T.B. line at Queen's Park Nº 3 signal box.' In addition, the points for the turnout on to the Bakerloo could not be cleared unless there was a Bakerloo train indicated in the train describer, or a train was stopped at signal QP4, which protects those points.

The extension to Stanmore changed things. Now there would be full-sized and tube-sized trains using the same tracks under largely automatic or remote-controlled signals. The risk of a Metropolitan Line train trying to enter the Bakerloo tunnels was much greater; something had to be done. The solution was to mount U-shaped tubes above the track, slightly higher than the roof of a tube train, north of Finchley Road on the southbound Bakerloo track. These tubes were full of mercury carrying an electric current. A Metropolitan Line train in the wrong place would smash the tubes, breaking the current and turning the next signal red; the train stop at the

signal would then bring the train to a stop. In more safety-conscious times, the mercury was replaced by conductive silver paint on the insides of the tubes. Now that the Jubilee Line uses automatic train operation and Metropolitan Line trains are banned, the tubes have been removed.

When the New Lines were resignalled in the 1980s, a new approach was taken. Approaching Queen's Park, there is a negative rail shoe detector 472m (516 yards) before signal WS8, which controls the junction on to the Bakerloo. The signal cannot clear for this direction unless a Bakerloo train is shown in the train describer and a negative shoe drawing current has been detected. WS37 and WS304 at Stonebridge Park similarly can't clear for routes into the depot unless a Bakerloo train is shown in the describer, something that regularly trips up inexperienced signallers.

Danger

Despite many safety mechanisms, incidents happen on railways ('accident' is hardly the right term for something that, usually, is caused by

No. 26 (left) and 25 (right) sidings at Queen's Park. LURS COLLECTION 01466

inattention or carelessness) and the Bakerloo is no exception.

At 08:19 on 8 October 1952, there was a double collision at Harrow & Wealdstone station when the driver of the overnight Perth express failed to brake at the distant signal, ran through two danger signals, and collided with the rear of a commuter train. Almost immediately, a train in the opposite direction ran into the wreckage. The engines of this last train ended up on the southbound New Lines track, where they cut off the current, stopping an approaching train from Watford. In total, 112 people were killed.

The Bakerloo has managed to avoid fatal incidents on passenger services, but there have been three significant ones on its trains. On 19 August 1949, two drivers were killed in a collision at Queen's Park between two 1938 Stock trains. One was intended to be put into siding 5 (now 25), while the other was waiting to come out of siding 6 (now 26), both in the south shed. However, the signalman made an error when writing down his instructions and sent the first train into siding 6. The driver realized too late and could not stop; a member of staff travelling with him was in hospital for two months. The signalman had not used a lever collar to warn him of the train in siding 6 (the rules did not require him to). It was recommended that the signal leading into the shed should indicate which siding the train was going into (this is now standard practice). Either of these would have prevented the incident.

Early in the morning of 25 September 1968, a 1938 Stock train came out of the south end of Neasden depot into the northbound Bakerloo platform, where the driver started to change ends ready to carry staff to Stanmore. As he and his guard were walking along the platform their train was hit by a ballast train that had run down the slope from Dollis Hill, passing through three red signals as it came. This train only had working brakes on the locomotive and the trainee driver – who died at the scene – had failed to control its speed properly. The report put most of the blame on the inspector who had accompanied him, but also noted the lack of speedometer in the driving cab. Both northbound tracks were blocked by the accident and services were badly disrupted all day.

Finally, on 7 July 1976 two 1938 Stock trains entered Neasden depot at the north end and were due to go to the washing plant. Both drivers ignored the stop board and instead accepted an unofficial hand signal from the shunter, not noticing that they had been sent down the wrong line. The first driver stopped behind a parked train, assuming there was a queue, then shut down his train and went home as his shift was up. The second driver accelerated too hard and crashed into the first train; both he and his guard (who was also in the cab) were killed. The shunter had failed to spot that the trains were on the wrong track, being too busy dealing with other problems in the area. Two other staff riding in the second train went off for a cup of tea rather than summoning help and failed to even report their presence at the scene. It turned out that working at the depot had become lax, with much rule-breaking being ignored.

There have been two very similar incidents involving the unusual New Lines signalling, the first on 16 October 1962 just north of Watford High Street station. After leaving Watford Junction there were six signals before the junction to Croxley Green: RWF33 (a repeater); WF33; RHS6 (another repeater); HS6 (which could also show a yellow aspect); HS4 (capable of showing both single and double yellows and fitted with 'directing' yellow lights on either side); and HS2/9, the High Street starting signal, with side by side signals for the Bushey and Croxley Green direction. The weather was foggy and signal HS4 had failed at red. The trains in question were the 10th and 11th of the seventeen due to run along this piece of track between 07:00 and 08:00. The first was a Bakerloo train, which had passed WF33 when the small yellow light had lit, stopped at RHS6, moved off after waiting a minute, then stopped behind a Croxley Green train waiting at HS6; the driver of this one received permission to pass the signal at danger. About thirty seconds later the rear of the Bakerloo train, which was still behind RHS6, was struck by a BR train to Euston. The driver claimed that the small yellow light of WF33 was lit as he approached, so he didn't need to stop. He was then unable to stop when he saw the Bakerloo train about a car-length away. The two rear cars of the Bakerloo train telescoped into each other, seriously injuring a married couple in one of them, while five

A Bakerloo train waits to depart Watford Junction; the platform 5 starting signal is visible at left. LURS COLLECTION 01413

other people received minor injuries. It turned out that the small yellow at WF33 was clearing fourteen seconds too early in normal circumstances, but thirty-two seconds too early if there were several trains close together (the circuit used a thermal relay, which needed to cool down), but this did not justify the BR driver's actions. Colonel Reed, who investigated the accident, suggested abolishing the special working with this aspect, but BR stated that it would not be able to run the service if it did. BR instead proposed modifying the system so that the driver would have to get out and push a button before the small yellow light would come on, but this was never put into practice. The two damaged cars were scrapped; one of them was the first '58' trailer to be withdrawn.

The second of these incidents happened exactly twenty-four years later, on the afternoon of 16 October 1986. A seven-car 1959 Stock train from Stonebridge Park was stopped at signal KG6, immediately before Kensal Green tunnel, when it was hit from behind by a BR train, almost destroying the rear car and damaging the next one badly. Twenty-eight of the forty-five passengers on the two trains, plus the two Bakerloo crew, were injured. The BR driver claimed that the previous signal, KG8, had changed from double red to red over yellow while he was waiting at it and then, about thirty seconds later, to plain yellow (the intermediate repeater RKG6 had been removed some months before because the wall it was mounted on was collapsing, so KG8 showed yellow, not green). Comprehensive testing of the signalling showed that this could not have happened and other technical evidence contradicted the driver's statement about his actions. Since the signalling was about to be replaced, only some minor recommendations were made.

Something applicable to both accidents was that the Bakerloo train came off much worse. This was because the solebars of the trains are at different heights, allowing the main-line train to slice through the body of the Bakerloo one. Another possible root cause is that, at many signals, the main aspect is higher than the roof of a Bakerloo train. In bad conditions the drivers of trains proceeding into an occupied line will naturally be looking for the signal and can literally overlook a Bakerloo train sitting in their way.

Other incidents on the Bakerloo over the years have, thankfully, been rather more minor and only a sample can be given here. On 25 February 1918, there was a collision at Warwick Avenue. Electrical problems had caused a number of signals to fail. Train 7 was standing in the southbound platform and train 29 had drawn up behind it with just the front half of the first car in the station. Three minutes later, train 1 ran into the back of it; the driver and two other members of staff suffered broken bones, while six passengers had minor injuries. There were two interrelated causes. First, the tail lamps on train 29 were switched off; staff shortages meant that nobody had checked them since the train left the sheds at Queen's Park. Second, at the time the rules required the conductor to walk ahead of a train that passed a red signal, where, as in this situation, curves meant that it was not possible to see the line ahead. The conductor had, instead, just ridden in the driving cab and it was clear from the damage that the train was going significantly faster than it should have been, meaning that when the driver and conductor finally saw train 29 it was too late.

Late at night on 17 August 1962, the southbound platform at Oxford Circus was treated to the sight of a man hanging upside-down by his legs from the coupling between two cars. It was assumed that he had been taken ill, or, perhaps, taken too much drink.

On the evening of 29 October 1975, a train derailed on the crossover at Piccadilly Circus. Clearing up the mess took most of the next day and, because the middle of the central section was blocked, a special service had to be operated. Two trains ran between Elephant & Castle and Trafalgar Square, one on each track, and similarly another pair ran between Oxford Circus and Baker Street, while a fifth ran on the southbound track between the latter and Swiss Cottage. Restricted services ran between Paddington and Queen's Park and between West Hampstead and Stanmore. Coaches also ran between Baker Street and West Hampstead.

1972 Stock car 3556 following a collision at Neasden depot on 22 May 1987.

R.J. GREENAWAY/LURS COLLECTION 07177

On 16 February 1980, a train derailed on the main lines at Bushey, with two coaches overturning and coming to rest on the New Lines; sixty-seven passengers were taken to hospital. Over the next three days, trains only ran as far north as Harrow & Wealdstone; since the reversing sidings had seen little use for some time, it turned out that the buffer stop lights were broken and needed replacing. On 18 February and early the following day BR ran a shuttle on the northbound track between Harrow and Watford High Street; beyond there, passengers had to walk or use the peak-hours Croxley Green service. On 20 February, a Bakerloo train finally ran from Watford Junction until Bushey, where it was discovered that the negative rail had not been reinstalled properly. The other three morning trains were therefore cancelled while the first one was taken out of service for careful checking. One train ran back that evening to ensure the numbers came out right, but it was not until 22 February that all was back to normal for the Bakerloo.

Late in the evening of 23 November 1984, a fire broke out in a storeroom at one end of the north-bound Victoria Line platform at Oxford Circus. Fourteen people were taken to hospital following smoke inhalation and various parts of the station suffered smoke damage, including the northbound Bakerloo platform and access tunnels. Northbound Bakerloo trains did not stop for the next six days while things were put right.

On 29 March 1994, a train overran the buffer stops in the Harrow reversing siding. Two cars had to be scrapped as a result. Finally, on 26 April 2012 there were press reports that one of the Bakerloo tunnels had collapsed south of Embankment. It turned out that heavy rain had cause excessive pressure in the clay around the tunnel and one of the iron rings had moved slightly; a train then grazed the resulting bulge.

CHAPTER 15

Future Plans

At the time of writing, TfL is considering extending the Bakerloo south-east once again, this time to Lewisham. The new line would branch off the existing one at Lambeth North and follow St George's Road to a new station under the eastern half of the Elephant & Castle intersection, heading along the New Kent Road. The existing separate Bakerloo and Northern Line entrances would be closed, replaced by a new one on the south-east corner. The route then follows the line of the New Kent Road, diverging off at Rodney Place and following a straight line to cross the Old Kent Road at Hendre Road, then turning to run under Marcia Road. Burgess Park station would be under the supermarket and car park at its east end. It then drifts across the Old Kent Road, with Asylum station in the 'V' formed by Asylum Road, then crosses the New Cross Road at All Saint's church before running under houses to New Cross Gate tube station, which is on the west side of the surface station and at an angle to it. It passes directly under the road bridge over the railway and then Goldsmiths College to the north side of St John's station, then curves gently south to the terminus, which is partly under the surface station at Lewisham and partly under the east end of Thurston Road. The tunnels finally curve round to just west of south to reach the Wearside Service Estate, a triangle formed by two railway lines and the Ravensbourne River. Stabling sidings would be built at basement level under this site.

If this proposal gets approval and funding, construction would start in 2023 and the line would open in 2029. An alternative route that reached New Cross Gate via Camberwell and Peckham Rye was also considered, but, in the end, not chosen. A second phase would see the line surface immediately after Lewisham and take over the existing line via Catford Bridge to Hayes, including the branch from New Beckenham to Beckenham Junction. The latter would allow the future possibility of a tunnel to Bromley town centre. Southwark Council is also pressing for an additional station at Bricklayer's Arms, roughly where the Old and New Kent Roads meet, though TfL has rejected this at least once.

An opposing proposal has come from the Canary Wharf Group, which owns much of the eponymous financial district. Their route would run via Surrey Quays and Canary Wharf itself to Charlton, implying two river crossings. However, the western half competes with the Jubilee Line and the eastern half with the Elizabeth Line, making it less attractive.

At the other end, the Bakerloo could be made to serve the HS2 station at Old Oak Common, either by a branch from Queen's Park or by a new tunnel loop from there to Willesden Junction, presumably removing Kensal Green from the line. TfL has also talked about removing all London Overground

Approaching Lewisham from the south; the line on the left would be taken over by the Bakerloo and the depot would be in the 'V'. (This photograph was taken during an authorized cab ride in a safe manner. Never trespass on railway lines to take images.)

services from north of Queen's Park and, therefore, returning the Bakerloo to Watford Junction once again; however, no concrete plans have been published. The Croxley Green branch was also going to be reused to let the Metropolitan Line reach Watford Junction, but after some preliminary work this now seems to have been abandoned.

Finally, moving to rolling stock, the Bakerloo is part of the 'New Tube for London' scheme to build new driverless trains for four tube lines – the others are the Central, Piccadilly, and Waterloo & City –

and, therefore, to replace the signalling. Siemens are building the first batch of ninety-four trains at a new factory in Goole, with delivery starting in 2023. However, the Bakerloo is at the end of the queue, with its new trains planned to arrive in the early 2030s and with no funding yet agreed. We could see the 1972 Stock still running in 2040.

Remember, though, that the history of the Bakerloo has shown that the future is always risky to predict, particularly when Camberwell is involved.

Line Diagram

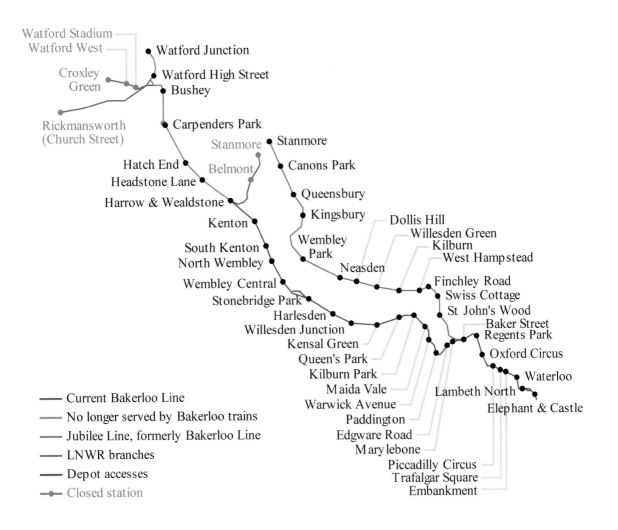

Watford Stadium
Watford West
Croxley Green
Rickmansworth (Church Street)

Watford Junction
Watford High Street
Bushey
Carpenders Park

Stanmore
Belmont

Stanmore
Canons Park
Queensbury
Kingsbury

Hatch End
Headstone Lane
Harrow & Wealdstone
Kenton
South Kenton
North Wembley
Wembley Central
Stonebridge Park
Harlesden
Willesden Junction
Kensal Green
Queen's Park
Kilburn Park
Maida Vale
Warwick Avenue
Paddington
Edgware Road
Marylebone

Wembley Park
Neasden

Dollis Hill
Willesden Green
Kilburn
West Hampstead
Finchley Road
Swiss Cottage
St John's Wood
Baker Street
Regents Park
Oxford Circus
Waterloo
Lambeth North
Elephant & Castle

Piccadilly Circus
Trafalgar Square
Embankment

—— Current Bakerloo Line
—— No longer served by Bakerloo trains
—— Jubilee Line, formerly Bakerloo Line
—— LNWR branches
—— Depot accesses
●—● Closed station

149

Appendix I Dates

Table I Station Opening Dates and Name Changes – Current Line

Station	Opened	Original name (if different)	Name change		Current name used from
Watford Junction*	5 May 1858				
Watford High Street	1 October 1862				
Bushey	1 December 1841		1 December 1912	Bushey & Oxhey	6 May 1974
Carpenders Park	1 April 1914				
Hatch End	1844		1 January 1897	Pinner & Hatch End	11 June 1956
			1 February 1920	Hatch End (for Pinner)	
Headstone Lane	10 February 1913				
Harrow & Wealdstone*	20 July 1837	Harrow Weald	1837	Harrow	1 May 1897
Kenton	15 June 1912		1927	Kenton for Northwick Park	Unknown
South Kenton	3 July 1933				
North Wembley	15 June 1912				
Wembley Central	1842	Sudbury	1 May 1882	Sudbury & Wembley	5 July 1948
			1 November 1910	Wembley for Sudbury	
Stonebridge Park	15 June 1912				
Harlesden	15 June 1912				
Willesden Junction	1 September 1866				
Kensal Green	1 October 1916				
Queen's Park	2 June 1879	Queen's Park (West Kilburn)			December 1954
Kilburn Park	31 January 1915				
Maida Vale	6 June 1915				
Warwick Avenue	31 January 1915				
Paddington	1 December 1913				
Edgware Road	15 June 1907				
Marylebone	27 March 1907	Great Central			15 April 1917
Baker Street	10 March 1906				
Regent's Park	10 March 1906				
Oxford Circus	10 March 1906				
Piccadilly Circus	10 March 1906				
Charing Cross	10 March 1906	Trafalgar Square			5 January 1979
Embankment	10 March 1906	Embankment	6 April 1914	Charing Cross (Embankment)	12 September 1976
			9 May 1915	Charing Cross	
			4 August 1974	Charing Cross Embankment	
Waterloo	10 March 1906				
Lambeth North	10 March 1906	Kennington Road	5 August 1906	Westminster Bridge Road	During 1928
			15 April 1917	Lambeth (North)	
Elephant & Castle	5 August 1906				

*The line opened as far as Hemel Hempstead on 20 July 1837. The original station in Watford was 565m (618 yards) north of the present one.

Table 2   Station Opening Dates and Name Changes – Stanmore Branch

Station	Opened	Original name (if different)	Name change		Current name used from
Stanmore	10 December 1932				
Canons Park	10 December 1932	Canons Park (Edgware)			During 1933
Queensbury	16 December 1934				
Kingsbury	10 December 1932				
Wembley Park	12 May 1894				
Neasden*	2 August 1880	Kingsbury & Neasden	1 January 1910	Neasden & Kingsbury	1 January 1932
Dollis Hill	1 October 1909		During 1931	Dollis Hill & Gladstone Park	During 1933
Willesden Green	24 November 1879		1 June 1894	Willesden Green & Cricklewood	During 1938
Kilburn	24 November 1879	Kilburn & Brondesbury			25 September 1950
West Hampstead	30 June 1879				
Finchley Road	30 June 1879		11 September 1885	Finchley Road (South Hampstead)	During 1914
Swiss Cottage	20 November 1939				
St John's Wood	20 November 1939				

* The line opened as far as Harrow-on-the-Hill on this date.
No station on the line has closed permanently. Carpenders Park moved to a new location on 17 November 1952, trains stopping at the old location for the last time the previous day.

Table 3   Stations Not Served by the Bakerloo Line Throughout their Lifetime

Station(s)	First served	Last day of service	Service resumed
Watford Junction to Headstone Lane except Carpenders Park	16 April 1917	24 September 1982	
Carpenders Park	5 May 1919	24 September 1982	
Harrow & Wealdstone to Wembley Central	16 April 1917	24 September 1982	4 June 1984
Stonebridge Park	1 August 1917		
Harlesden	16 April 1917		
Willesden Junction	10 May 1915		
Queen's Park	11 February 1915		
Stanmore to St John's Wood	20 November 1939	30 April 1979	

Table 4   Temporary Closures

Only temporary closures lasting at least a week are shown. Where a section of line was closed, stations named in [brackets] remained open. Events on the Stanmore branch after the opening of the Jubilee Line are not listed.

Last day of service before closure	Date reopened	Section or station	Reason
31 December 1916	5 May 1919	Carpenders Park	Wartime restrictions
9 January 1917	1 August 1917	Stonebridge Park	Fire damage
27 September 1938	8 October 1938	[Piccadilly Circus] to Elephant & Castle	Underwater tunnels plugged because of war risk
31 August 1939	20 November 1939	Oxford Circus (street access only; interchange still possible)	Floodgate installation
31 August 1939	17 December 1939	Embankment	Floodgate installation

Table 4 *(continued)*

Last day of service before closure	Date reopened	Section or station	Reason
31 August 1939	9 January 1940	Maida Vale	Floodgate installation
16 January 1941	21 April 1941	[Waterloo] to Elephant & Castle	Bomb damage at Lambeth North
13 August 1944	25 August 1944	[Piccadilly Circus] to Elephant & Castle	Repairs
24 June 1990	28 January 1992	Edgware Road	Lift replacement
10 November 1996	14 July 1997	[Piccadilly Circus] to Elephant & Castle	Tunnel strengthening
3 March 1997	15 March 1997	[Oxford Circus] to [Piccadilly Circus] (northbound trains ran empty, southbound trains in passenger service)	Derailment
22 October 1999	1 November 1999	Harrow & Wealdstone to [Queen's Park]*	Track replacement
29 October 1999	10 November 1999	Stonebridge Park	Building work
28 January 2001	17 February 2001	Edgware Road	Lift repairs
1 September 2002	13 January 2003 evenings 3 February 2003 off-peak 2 May 2003 fully open	Baker Street (northbound only, weekdays only)	Escalator repairs
22 November 2002	30 November 2002	Edgware Road, Regent's Park, [Waterloo] to Elephant & Castle	Firefighters' strike
22 October 2004	1 November 2004	Harrow & Wealdstone to [Queen's Park]*	Engineering works
10 July 2006	13 June 2007	Regent's Park	Lift replacement
24 December 2009	4 January 2010	[Stonebridge Park] to [Queen's Park]	Engineering works
24 May 2013	21 December 2013	Edgware Road	Lift replacement
7 January 2014	1 November 2014	Embankment	Escalator replacement
1 April 2016	1 August 2016	Paddington	Elizabeth Line work
12 July 2016	13 February 2017	Lambeth North	Lift replacement

* Other rail services continued to operate between Watford Junction and Stonebridge Park on the New Lines during both these closures.

Appendix II   Proposed Names

In some cases the name that a station was given during the planning stage is not the one it opened with.

Table 5   Proposed Names

Station(s)	Original proposed name(s)
Kilburn Park	Kilburn
Maida Vale	Elgin Avenue
Warwick Avenue	Warrington Crescent
Marylebone	Lisson Grove *or* Marylebone
Kingsbury	Kingsbury Green
St John's Wood	Acadia Road *then* Acacia

Appendix III   Station Locations and Layouts

For explanations of Grid, Ongar, Heights and Layout, *see* after the table. Note: italics indicate locations other than stations.

Table 6   Station Locations and Layouts

Station	Location		Height above sea level		Layout
	Grid	Ongar	Platform (NB/SB)	Surface	
Main line					
Watford Junction	110 973	74.18			X1
Watford High Street	113 960	72.79			IP
Bushey	118 952	71.52			OP-6
Carpenders Park (original)	118 935	69.39			OP
Carpenders Park (present)	119 934	69.37			IP
Hatch End	130 914	67.12			OP
Headstone Lane	139 905	65.91			OP
Harrow & Wealdstone	154 894	64.00		52	OP-6
Kenton	167 883	62.26		56	OP
South Kenton	173 870	60.86		43	IP
North Wembley	176 862	59.96		48	OP
Wembley Central	182 851	58.69		45	OP-6
Stonebridge Park	196 842	56.98		24	OP
Harlesden	209 834	55.45		38	OP
Willesden Junction	219 829	54.40		40	X2
Kensal Green	233 828	52.90		42	OP
Boundary between NR and LU	243 831	51.81			
Queen's Park	245 832	51.58		38	D1
Tunnel mouth	248 833	51.28			
Kilburn Park	253 833	50.78	19.5	27	CP
Maida Vale	259 827	49.89	16.6	31	CP
Warwick Avenue	261 820	49.11	12.5	27	CP
Paddington	265 813	48.24	9.3	25	CP
Edgware Road	271 817	47.51	7.1	32	OP
Marylebone	274 819	47.05	6.4	29	OP
Baker Street	280 820	46.55	8.3/5.1*	27	X3
Regent's Park	287 822	45.67	4.2	28	WP
Oxford Circus	290 812	44.80	4.7	27	X4
Piccadilly Circus	296 806	43.83	−6.2	19	OP
Trafalgar Square	300 804	43.28	−11.8	12	CP
Embankment	303 803	42.91	−14.9	5	OP
Waterloo	309 800	42.44	−14.9/−11.8	4	EP
Depot access junction	310 794	41.72			
Lambeth North	312 794	41.57	−13.3/−13.7	3	CP
Elephant & Castle	319 791	40.74	−19.8	3	CP
End of northbound tunnel	320 789	40.44			
End of southbound tunnel	320 788	40.38			
Stanmore branch					
Stanmore	175 925	64.62	76.8	85	X5
Canons Park	181 912	63.27	70.1	65	OP
Queensbury	188 897	61.56	51.2	48	OP
Kingsbury	193 886	60.23	38.3	43	OP
Wembley Park	193 863	57.38	36.7	41	OP-6
Neasden	213 853	55.09	32.2	38	IP-4

Table 6 (continued)

Station	Location		Height above sea level		Layout
	Grid	Ongar	Platform (NB/SB)	Surface	
Dollis Hill	222 851	54.24	39.4	37	IP
Willesden Green	233 848	53.03	50.3	56	IP-4
Kilburn	245 846	51.84	52.2	45	IP
West Hampstead	256 846	50.75	50.5	56	IP
Finchley Road	261 848	50.14	48.7	52	D2
Swiss Cottage	266 843	49.53	40.1	57	CP
St John's Wood	267 833	48.61	31.2/31.7	49	CP
Stonebridge Park depot					
End of longest depot track	187 846	58.04			
Access line NR/LU boundary	194 843	57.16		(24)	
London Road depot					
Depot tunnel mouth	315 793	41.30	(−0.3)	4	
End of longest depot track	317 793	40.99	(−0.3)	4	
Croxley Green branch (from Bushey)					
Colne Junction	113 955	72.08			
Croxley Junction	109 955	72.71			
Watford Stadium	103 954	73.19			SP
Watford West	098 956	73.69			NP
Croxley Green	088 958	74.84			NP
Croxley Green branch connection (from Watford High Street)					
Watford High Street Junction	111 958	72.55			
Croxley Junction	109 955	71.90			

* The southbound platform on the Stanmore branch, now the eastbound Jubilee Line platform, is at 4.3.

Grid: this is the location based on the Ordnance Survey National Grid, with the prefix 'TQ' omitted. A location '123 456' means a 100m square that is 12.3km east of and 45.6km north of a reference point just off the coast between Bognor Regis and Littlehampton. Locations around the Bakerloo Line are as follows (note that, because the grid is defined using a Transverse Mercator projection, grid directions are not exactly the same as those found on a globe):

100 900 0°24'48"W 51°35'53"N	200 900 0°16'08"W 51°35'46"N	300 900 0°07'29"W 51°35'38"N
100 800 0°24'59"W 51°30'30"N	200 800 0°16'20"W 51°30'22"N	300 800 0°07'42"W 51°30'14"N
100 700 0°25'10"W 51°25'06"N	200 700 0°16'33"W 51°24'59"N	300 700 0°07'55"W 51°24'51"N

Ongar: distances along Underground lines are measured in kilometres using 'distance from Ongar'. On the surface, it is possible to see the white kilometre posts with black numbers and smaller posts with a single digit at intermediate 200m intervals. This system is based on a survey done in 1972. At the time, Ongar was one of the furthest Underground stations from central London (it is no longer an Underground station, but is one end of the Epping and Ongar preservation line) and,

Ongar distance sign on a wall at Willesden Green station.

unlike the other candidates, was a terminus with no likelihood of extension. Therefore distances on the Central Line (other than the Hainault loop) are measured directly from the buffer stops at Ongar, while for all other lines the distances are 'transferred' at some convenient point where the lines run parallel or on the same tracks. Branches facing the wrong way therefore have distances that count downwards. In the case of the Bakerloo, the distances transfer from the Central to the District at

Mile End, then follow the District and Piccadilly to Rayners Lane. They then count down along the Metropolitan and then Jubilee to Baker Street, before finally transferring across to the Bakerloo at the junction of the southbound tracks. According to Transport for London, the Ongar system is no longer used.

Heights: these are relative to the Ordnance Survey reference datum at Newlyn. Plain numbers are based on official sources; those in parentheses have been interpolated or determined in other ways.

Between Bushey and Wembley Central the tracks used by the Bakerloo are on the west side of the four main-line tracks. Between Willesden Junction and Queen's Park they are on the north side of the four main-line tracks. Between Wembley Park and Finchley Road they are between the Metropolitan Line tracks, with the ex-GCR lines to the west without platforms. Unless indicated otherwise, there are no platforms on the main line or Metropolitan tracks.

Layout codes:

CP	Two separate platform tunnels with platforms between the tracks connected by cross-passages.
D1	Two island platforms with the Bakerloo between them and the tracks of the New Lines on the outside. The two nearest main-line tracks on the northbound side have disused platforms outside them.
D2	Two island platforms with the Bakerloo between them and the tracks of the Metropolitan on the outside.
EP	Two separate platform tunnels with platforms on the east side in each case.
IP	Island platform between the tracks.
IP-4	Island platform between the tracks and platforms outside the Metropolitan Line tracks.
NP	Single track with platform on the north side.
OP	Platforms outside the tracks.
OP-6	Two outside platforms and two island platforms.
SP	Single track with platform on the south side.
WP	Two separate platform tunnels with platforms on the west side in each case.
X1	Four terminal platforms with two peninsular platforms on the west side of four through platforms and a bay on the main line and one platform on the St Albans branch.
X2	Island platform with a south-facing bay between the through tracks. The main lines are to the west.
X3	See figure on p.102.
X4	Originally OP. The Victoria Line platform tunnels were added outside the Bakerloo ones, connected to them by cross-passages.
X5	Three terminal platforms with a peninsular platform between the eastern two and one outside the western one. Sidings on the east side.

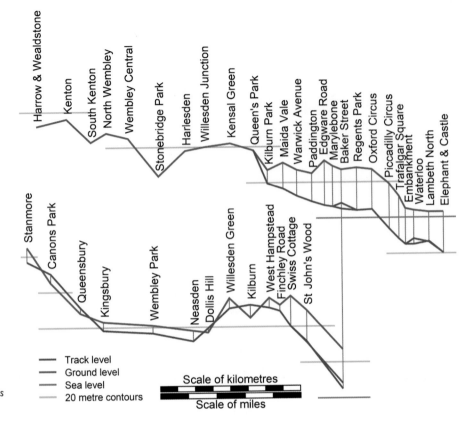

Cross-section of the Bakerloo Line (track heights are not available beyond Queen's Park).

Track level
Ground level
Sea level
20 metre contours

Scale of kilometres

Scale of miles

Index

1906 Stock 60, 115–119
1914 Stock 117–119
1920 Stock 120–121
1935 Stock 123
1938 Stock 60, 66, 100, 121, 123–131, 141, 143–144
1949 Stock 125–126
1959 Stock 128–129, 145
1967 Stock 44, 129
1972 Stock 125, 129–130, 146, 148
'58 trailers' 121, 123, 126, 145

'A' and 'D' 124–125, 130
accidents 143–146
Acton Works 120, 127, 129–130
Acts and Bills, BS&WR 23, 25–26, 28–29, 33, 39, 54, 56, 59
    other companies 25, 55, 59, 68
    predecessors 15, 18–19
    procedure 16
    recent 74–75, 101, 106
Addington 70
air raids 69, 89–91
air shafts 43
air-powered doors 120–121, 125
Albany Road 74
Alderney 128–129
Aldwych 90, 96, 101
Alpine orogeny 21–22
aluminium 128
American Car & Foundry Co. 116
Andreoni, M. and Mlle 33
arcing 116
Asylum 147
Australian mining companies 27, 31
Austria-Hungary 116
automatic train operation 130, 142

babies 72
Baker Street 30, 41, 53, 72, 75, 99, 156
    decorations 83, 102
    layout 41, 43, 81–82, 102
    lifts and escalators 57, 97, 113
    on routes 24–26, 29, 39, 55, 70, 76–81, 101–102
    passengers 26, 30, 54, 104
    rebuilding 45, 53, 81, 102
    services 39, 79, 145
    signalling and control 138–139
    substation 47

Baker Street & Waterloo Railway 23–31, 33–34, 37–39, 41–42, 51, 55
Bakerloo Harrow cars 123
Bakerloo name 42
ban on railways 11–13
Bank 10–11, 21–24, 30, 96, 109
Bank of England 15, 33, 75
Barking 104
Barlow, Peter 20–21
Baudry, Stanislaus 11
Beach, Alfred Ely 16, 20
bearer bonds 75
Beck, Harry 75
Beckenham Junction 147
Bentley Prior 78
Berlin 17
Bigham, Mr Justice 33–34
Billy Brown 92
Birmingham Railway Carriage & Wagon Co. 121, 123
Blackfriars 10, 18
blackmail 35–36
blackout 90
block system 135
blue stripe 74, 123
boarding controls 70
bombing 69, 88–89, 92–94, 99, 112
Bond Street 101
Borrowed Stock 55, 118–119
Bound, Arthur Frank 134–135
bribery 32, 36
Bricklayers Arms 147
Bright's disease 39
British America Corporation 32
British Pneumatic Railway Signal Company 135
British Rail(ways) 95, 98, 106, 108–109
British Thomson–Houston 116
British Transport Commission 95–97, 101
British Transport stock 95
Broad Street 59, 61, 67, 91, 98
Bromley 108, 147
Brompton & Piccadilly Circus Railway 36
Brondesbury 55, 59
Browne, Florence 33
Brunel, Marc Isambard 20–21
Brush Electrical Engineering Co. 117–118
buffer-stop collisions 146
Burgess Park 147

buses 7, 11–14, 23–24, 29
Bushey 63, 67, 98–99, 136, 146, 156

cabs 11–12, 14, 24, 29
Camberwell 10, 74, 96–98, 125, 147–148
Camden 10, 58–59, 117, 134–135
Cammell Laird & Co. Ltd 118, 120–121
camshaft 124
Canary Wharf 147
Cannon Street 10, 101
Canons Park 86, 99, 129
capital, company 15–16, 18, 25–27, 29, 31, 36–37, 39
Capitalcard 109
car 10306 126–127
Carpenders Park 66–67, 96
CCTV 103, 112
Central London Railway/Central Line 19, 24, 42, 51, 52, 72, 89, 97, 101, 106, 112, 118, 128, 141, 148, 156
Channel Tunnel 23, 78
Chapman, James 41
Charing Cross 8, 10, 16, 24–25, 29–30, 102, 105, 112
Charing Cross, Euston, & Hampstead railway 36
Charing Cross & Waterloo Electric Railway 17–19
Charlton 147
Chelsea 38, 54
Chicago 7, 35–36, 40, 115
Chicago Traction Wars 36
Chiltern Hills 22, 57
Chiswick 54
Circle Line/Inner Circle 22–23, 25, 29–30, 49, 52, 54, 56, 77, 79, 106–107
circle-and-bar 50–51
City & South London Railway (also see Northern Line) 23–24, 29, 47, 51, 74
City Terminus Company 12–13
Clark, Charles Walter 84–86
Clark, Josiah 13
classes of seating 15, 18, 26, 41
Cochrane, Admiral Lord 20
College Street 14, 17, 42
collisions 135, 139, 143–146
Colne Junction 65, 134–135
Commandos 125
compensation 15, 24, 30, 117
compressed air 38

Connor, Piers 116
construction, costs and funding 15, 18–19, 25, 29
  progress 15–16, 19, 28, 30, 38–39, 60–61
contactless payment 109–110
contactor 116
control equipment 116–117, 123–124
control trailers 116–117, 119–121
coshes 125
coupler 124, 128–129
Couronnes disaster 39
Cowperwood, Frank 36, 40
cricket fans 7, 23, 41
Cricklewood 55
Croxley Green 65–66, 91, 99, 103, 108, 120, 124,
  126, 136, 139, 146, 148
Croxley Junction 65–66
Crystal Palace 14, 17, 82, 112
cut and cover 13, 15, 17, 22, 25, 79
cyanide 34

de-icing 93, 141
deadman (handle) 126, 140
debt 97, 99
decimal currency 8, 99
Denmark Hill 74
derailments 145–146
Dickens & Jones 70
dinosaurs 21
District Line 22, 29, 36, 37–38, 45, 46, 47, 52,
  67, 77, 96, 101, 106, 111–112, 115, 120, 128,
  132, 156
diveunder 81, 86
dividends 15, 18, 23, 29, 31–32, 35–38, 47, 70,
  75, 90
Docklands Light Railway 104
docks 57, 59, 104
Dollis Hill 81, 84–85, 143
door interlock circuit 120
double-glazed door 125
double-leaf doors 120–121, 125
Dreiser, Theodore 36, 40
DRICO 140–141
driver(s) 47, 70, 104, 112, 116–117, 120, 124,
  129–130, 135, 140–145
driverless trains 148
driving controls 115–116, 140
Dufferin, Marquess of 27, 31
Dunn, Samuel 21
Dunton Road 112

East and West India Docks and Birmingham
  Junction Railway 59
East London Line 26, 59, 101, 106, 112
Ebury, Baron 58
Edgware 79
'Edmund Burke', loco 77
electric trains, history 17–18, 23–24
electrical problems 47, 52, 145
electrification 17, 29, 37–38, 46, 58, 60, 66, 78,
  115, 118, 120
  four rail 52, 99, 108
Elephant and Castle 13, 15, 26, 29, 30, 33, 42, 46,
  47, 48–49 55, 59, 70, 72, 74, 81, 94, 98, 107,
  111, 113, 114, 117, 121, 123, 128, 130, 132,
  138–139, 141, 145, 147
  sidings 44, 74
Elizabeth Line 29, 70, 113, 147
Embankment 8, 14, 17, 30, 43, 45, 47, 52, 69, 70,
  71, 79, 89, 92, 96, 99, 113, 138, 146
Eocene 22
EP brakes 122–124
Eros 74
escalators 52, 53, 56, 62, 70–71, 72, 73, 81,
  82, 91–92, 93, 96, 97, 98, 102–103, 105,
  110–111, 113

power saving 97
shaft digging 70, 98
shunt and comb 56–57, 71
Eurostar 105
Euston 10, 12, 14, 25, 26, 28–29, 33, 57, 58, 59,
  61, 67, 91, 98, 99, 104, 114, 134–135
Euston loop 58
Euston Road 10, 25–26, 30, 77
Evening News 42

fares 15, 18, 24, 29, 41, 47, 70–71, 89, 100,
  107–108, 110
  Metropolitan v LER 79
  through 46–47
  workmen 41, 51, 71
  zones 107–108
Fares Fair 107
Farringdon 13
'Felthams' 121, 123
female staff 59, 90
Fenchurch Street 10, 59, 96, 101, 104
finances, World War II 90
financial problems 13, 15, 25, 38, 50, 59, 75, 97,
  99, 108
Finchley Road 78–83, 91, 138, 141–142, 156
fire 39, 66, 96, 113, 130, 146
firefighters strike 113
flag switch 122
Fleet Street 10, 101
Fliegender Hamburger 123
flooding and floodgates 69, 88–90, 138
fluorescent lighting 128
fog repeaters 138
food train 91
frost 67, 93

gate stock (*also see* 1906 and 1914 Stocks) 116,
  118, 121
gauge 12, 24, 38
Ghostbusters II 16
Gibb, Sir George 50
Gloucester Railway Carriage & Wagon Co. 121
Golders Green 58
Gordon, Frederick 78
Grant, President Ulysses 35
Great Central Railway 25–26, 29, 47, 54, 78,
  135, 156
Great Eastern Railway 17
Great Northern, Piccadilly, & Brompton Railway
  39
Great Northern & City Railway 24, 51
Great Northern & Strand Railway 36
Great Northern Railway 12
Great Scotland Yard 14
Great Western Railway 29, 54–57, 91
Greater London Authority 106–107
Greater London Council 99–100, 104, 106–107,
  129
Greathead, James 20–21
Green, Leslie William 44, 46, 49, 61, 74, 82, 113
Green Park 96, 101, 105
Grouping 59, 71, 75
guards 47, 51, 90, 111–112, 116–117, 119–121,
  140, 143–145

H.P. White 59
Hackney 10, 59
Hagger, Police Constable Joseph Corr 66
Hale, Professor George 40
Hammersmith & City Line 13, 77, 106
Hampstead 24, 59
Hampstead, St. Pancras & Charing Cross Railway
  24
Hampstead line (*also see* Northern Line) 36, 47,
  52, 54, 58, 71, 116, 120
handgrips 124–125
Harlesden 63, 110, 136

Harrow, town 57, 76
Harrow & Wealdstone 6, 57–58, 60, 63, 74, 79,
  90, 91, 96, 99, 108–109, 111, 114, 123, 134,
  143, 146
Harrow-on-the-Hill 58, 75, 78, 150
Hatch End 57, 63–64, 135
Hayes 147
Headstone Lane 64, 67
Heaps, Stanley Arthur 62, 82, 86
heaters 119
Hemel Hempstead 150
Herne Hill 96
Holborn 10, 12, 14, 19
Hornblower, Horatio 20
Horsley, Gerald 63
housing 10, 63, 72, 75, 78, 86, 96
'Hungarian' stock 116, 118
Hungerford Bridge 13–14, 18–19, 27–28
Hyde Park Corner 54–55
hydraulic rams 20, 38
income sharing 75, 89
Institution of Railway Signal Engineers 135
insulated block joint 133
intercom 121, 140
interest (money) 15, 18, 31, 35–37, 59, 97
Interlocking Machine Rooms 139
Intersection Tunnel 63
Island Line, Isle of Wight 128

John, Elton 68
Jubilee Gardens 14, 42
Jubilee Line 101–106, 126, 129–130, 139,
  141–142, 147, 156
  name change 104
junction construction 102

Kensal Green and tunnels 60–62, 92, 145, 147
Kensington 11, 77
Kenton 58, 67, 76, 123
Kew 59, 61
Kilburn 10, 23, 55, 79, 83–84, 93, 96, 101,
  135
Kilburn High Road 99–100
Kilburn Park 59, 61–62, 67, 71–72, 110
kilometre posts 156
King's Cross 10, 12, 19, 25, 130
King's Cross, Charing Cross & Waterloo Subway
  19
Kingsbury 72, 86

'La Lorraine' 33
Lambeth Group 22
Lambeth North 39, 41–42, 44, 46, 88, 92, 98, 107,
  111, 132, 134, 138–139 147
lawsuits 33, 38
Leeds Forge Company 117, 121
Lewisham 96, 101, 112, 147–148
lift shafts 30, 48, 57, 70, 102
lifts 25, 39, 41, 45–46, 49, 53, 62, 111, 113
  replacement 53, 70–71, 73, 110–111
  technical details 45–46, 70
  wedding story 91
Lillie Bridge depot 120
line controller 140–141
Lisson Grove 58
litter bins removed 99
liveries 74, 116, 119, 123, 130
Liverpool Street 10, 24, 56, 59
Livingstone, Kenneth Robert 106
locomotives 13–14, 17–18, 38, 68, 77, 115–116,
  143
London, history 10
  population 10, 23
London, Brighton, & South Coast Railway 26,
  135
London & Birmingham Railway 57, 59
London and Blackwall Railway 59

London and Globe Finance Corporation 27–29, 31–33
  crash and investigation 31–32
London and North Eastern Railway 78, 83
London and North Western Railway 57–59, 62–64, 67–68, 72, 79, 99, 117–120, 134, 141–142
London and South Western Railway 15, 26, 29, 31, 99
London Bridge 10, 12, 26, 72, 105
London Central Electric Railway 19
London Clay 21–22, 24, 27, 70
London County Council 24, 39, 41, 117
London Electric Railways 51, 56, 70, 79, 118–121, 142
London General Omnibus Company 51
London Midland and Scottish Railway 72, 91, 120, 135, 142
London Passenger Transport Board 75, 78–79, 82, 89–90, 95, 120, 123
London Rail Plan 98
London Regional Transport 106
London Road depot 26, 29, 37–38, 42, 43–44, 47, 86, 88, 92, 93–94, 103, 117, 122, 132, 134
London Transport 100, 129
  shares 75, 95
London Transport Board 97, 99
London Transport Executive (1948–1962) 95, 97, 125–126
London Transport Executive (1970–1984) 99, 106, 129
London Transport Museum Depot 128
London Transport wartime propaganda 92
London United Tramways 47
Lord, Thomas 82
Lord's Cricket Ground 23–24, 79–82
Lords (station) 81
Lots Road 38–39, 47
loudspeakers 92
Ludgate Circus 96, 101

Maida Vale 50, 59, 61, 63, 67, 89
maps 51, 75
Marble Arch 55, 96
Mare Crisium 40
marker light codes 120, 130–131
Marlborough Road 81
Marylebone 11, 26, 41, 43, 45, 47–48, 54, 78–81, 93, 96, 97, 132
  extension to 47
May, Frank Boyd 33–34
Medhurst, George 13
Metronet 106
Metropolitan Railway/Line (also see North Metropolitan Railway) 15, 30, 50, 53, 54, 55, 70, 75, 77, 78, 79, 84–86, 106, 120, 123, 156
  branches 78
  competition with Bakerloo 30, 58, 66, 72, 76
  effects of Bakerloo Stanmore branch 81, 83, 86–87
  Great Central connection 25, 78
  history and expansion 13, 22, 51, 72, 77–79
  objections to competition 25, 29, 54–56, 68, 75
  signalling 79–81, 138–139, 142
  technology 15, 46
  track rearrangements 79–81, 83, 86
  Watford branch 68, 72, 78, 148
Metropolitan Board of Works 18
Metropolitan–Cammell Carriage & Wagon Co. Ltd 121, 123, 130
Metropolitan Carriage, Wagon & Finance Co. 119, 121
Middlesex 55, 82
miners and tunnelling teams 20–21, 38
money, equivalents over time 8

motor car(s) 60, 115–126, 128–129
motor-generator 124
motors 17, 41, 116, 118, 120, 122–123, 125, 128–129
multiple–unit control 115

Nantes 11
Napoleon 20
National Liberal Club 16, 24
nationalization 75, 95
Neasden 81, 84–86, 125, 143, 146
Neasden depot 84–86, 103, 138, 143–144
negative rail 52, 100, 108, 146
negative rail shoe detector 142
New Cross (Gate) 49, 101, 112, 147
New Cross and Waterloo Railway 26, 29
New Kent Road 26, 147
New Lines 58–60, 62–63, 65, 74, 103, 122, 134–135, 143, 146
New Lines signalling 135–138, 139, 142, 144, 145
New Road (also see Euston Road) 10–13
New Tube for London stock 148
Nichols, Captain George Herbert Fosdike 42
non-driving motor (NDM) 124, 126, 128
non-stopping 67, 90
North & South Western Junction Railway 59
North Acton 112
North Downs 22
North London Railway/Line 59, 61, 63, 136
North Metropolitan Railway (also see Metropolitan Railway) 12–13
North Wembley 67
North West London Railway 55
Northern Line 23–24, 89, 102, 105–106, 121, 125, 128–130, 147
Northumberland Avenue 17, 19, 24, 30, 43

observatory 40
Oerlikons 66
Old Colony Trust 37, 50
Old Kent Road 26, 112, 147
Old Oak Common 147
One Person Operation ('OPO') 112, 140
Ongar system 156
Operation Pied Piper 90
Orsman, Mark 130
Otis lifts and escalators 46, 56–57, 62, 71–72
overcrowding 51, 69
Overend, Gurney, and Co. 15
overhauls 120, 128
overhead wires 38
overlap, signalling 132, 135
Oxford Circus 24–25, 29, 30, 38–39, 43, 46, 70, 73, 97, 99, 104, 111, 113, 145–146
  reconstructions 39, 52–53, 57, 72, 89, 97
Oxford Street 10
Oyster 109–110

Paddington 10, 12, 54, 57, 61, 79, 91, 107, 111, 113, 134, 138, 145
  extension to 28–30, 33, 54–56, 59
Paris 33, 39, 78, 130
Parliament (also see Acts and Bills) 11–13, 19, 23–24, 26, 29, 33–34, 41, 55, 82
Parliamentary committee 16, 24, 29
Parliamentary deposit 16, 36–37
Parliamentary process 16, 116
Pascal, Blaise 11
passenger door controls 125, 128
passenger protests 98, 100
passimeter 71–72, 98, 108
Pearson, Charles 12
Peckham 98, 101, 103, 147
Perry & Co. 27, 38
Piccadilly Circus 8, 23, 30, 32, 38, 43, 45, 46–47, 70, 73, 88, 92, 111, 112, 113, 118, 134, 138, 145

Piccadilly Line 36, 39, 45, 47, 51, 55, 67, 73, 101, 106, 116–118, 120, 123, 126, 128–129, 138, 148, 156
Frank Pick 32, 70, 75
pipe subway 73
platform extension 75
platform heights 67, 118
Pneumatic Dispatch Company 13
pneumatic railway 13–14, 16–17, 20
poison 34
ponies 38
pooled receipts 75, 89
Post Office 14, 19
power stations and supply 24, 38–39, 47, 58, 67, 103
prices, equivalents over time 8
Primrose Hill 58–59, 61
privatization 106
proposed branches and extensions 26, 28–29, 33, 112, 147
proposed new tube lines 70, 74
prospectus 15, 18, 29, 47
Public–Private Partnerships 106–107
publicity 50

Queen's Park 58, 59, 60, 61, 67, 69, 74, 81, 91, 99, 98, 101, 104, 112, 117–118, 121, 123, 141, 143, 145, 147, 156
  depot 60, 62, 86, 103, 127
  extension to 59, 62, 70
  signalling 133–134, 138, 141–142
Queensbury 86–87, 99
Quex 42

racks, hat and parcel 119
Rammell, Thomas 13–14, 16
Read, E.B. 33–34
Regent's Park 43, 45–46, 51, 58, 67, 108–111
  station ban 24–25, 39
repeater signal 111, 135, 138, 144–145
Richmond 59, 61, 63, 67, 99
Rickmansworth 58, 65–66, 78, 120
ring, tunnel 20–22, 38, 92, 146
River Line 104
R.M.S. Oceanic 33
R.M.S. Titanic 33
Rotherhithe New Road 112
route description 42–43, 61–63, 65, 81, 83–86

Scientific American 16
screw jacks 20, 38
searchlight signal 134, 138
seating 14, 60, 116–117, 119–121, 125, 130
segments, tunnel 20–21, 69, 92
semaphore signals 134, 138
service levels 29, 41, 47, 60–61, 69, 74, 79, 81, 87, 94, 97–98, 100, 104, 108, 113–114, 121
services 18, 55, 81, 87, 114, 117–118
  beyond Queen's Park 61, 66–67, 74, 91, 98–99, 108, 114, 123, 148
  exceptional situations 92, 113, 145–146
Sevenoaks 70
Shell Centre 16, 42, 96, 105
Shepherd's Plaid 22
Sherlock Holmes 102–103
shield, tunnelling 20–22, 38, 62, 141
shipworm 20
Siemens, Carl Wilhelm 18–19
Siemens, Werner von 17–18
Siemens/Siemens Brothers 18–19, 148
signal box diagram 132–133, 139
signal boxes 41, 81, 132–135, 138–140, 142
signal failures 135, 144
signalling 89, 132–139, 148
  LU 138
  Mirfield 135
signals, automatic 132, 135–136, 142

sleet and snow 67–68, 93
South Eastern Railway 20, 25, 78
South Hampstead 135
South Kenton 75, 98
Southern Railway 75
speed 14–15, 18, 30, 41, 92, 118, 121–122, 132, 138, 143
speed signalling 135
speed–control signals 138
Speyer, Sir Edgar 37, 50
Speyer Brothers 37, 47
spoil removal lawsuit 38
Sprague, Frank Julian 115
sprung doors 117
St John's Wood 2, 23, 70–71, 81–83
St Katharine Docks 104
St Paul's (station) 19, 83
St Paul's Cathedral 14, 82
Stabler, Harold 82–83
stabling facilities 86, 93, 147
Standard Exploration Company 31–32
Standard Stock 121–123, 128, 131
Stanley, Albert Henry 50–51, 70–72, 75, 95
Stanmore and branch 7, 58, 77–81, 86–88, 93–94, 97–98, 101–103, 106, 121, 125, 130, 138, 141–143, 145
Stanmore branch (LNWR) 58, 78
Starlight Express 128
state control 89, 95
stations, decorations 45, 56, 63, 73, 84, 102, 111–113
    descriptions 61–63, 65, 73–74, 82–86
    design 45–46, 48–49, 52
    design, 'country bungalow' 63–64
    names 8
    proposed closures 108
    rebuilding and upgrades 39, 65–66, 71–73, 83, 93, 96–98, 102, 105–106, 109, 111, 113
    tiles 84
Stonebridge Park 63, 66–67, 96, 103–104, 108, 111, 124, 128, 134, 139
Stonebridge Park depot 63, 103–104, 108, 139
Strand (road) 10, 101
Strand (station) 102
Stratford 105
Streamline Moderne 83–84
substations 47, 52, 67, 128, 140
suffragettes 66
Surrey Docks/Quays 101, 104, 147
Susan Sensible 92
Swan & Edgar 70
swing doors 119
Swiss Cottage 77, 79–83, 145

telescope 40
Teredo navalis 20
terrorist attacks 99
Thames, diverting 104
    geology 37
    pier 27
Thames tunnel 14–15, 17, 28, 88, 146
    armour plating 69, 92, 112
    plugged 88
Thames tunnel (Tower Subway) 20, 38
Thames tunnel (Wapping) 20, 101
Thamesmead 104

ticket gates 108–110
ticket machines 73, 109
ticket offices 49, 71, 98
    abolition and reuse 110
ticketing systems 108–110
tickets, through 46–47
tiles and tiling 11, 39, 45, 82–83, 85, 113
Tottenham Court Road 15, 49
Tower Subway 20, 38
track circuits 52, 132–135
track rearrangements 80–81, 83, 86, 108–109
'Traction' company 36–37
traction interlock 120
Trafalgar Square 8, 11, 12, 17, 19, 29–30, 41, 43, 45–46, 70, 71, 92–93, 96, 101–102, 104–105, 107, 111–112, 145
traffic 25–26, 30, 47, 51, 56, 57, 59, 63, 70, 74–75, 79, 87, 90–91, 94, 97, 100, 101, 105, 108, 134
    road 12, 23–24, 73, 97
trailer cars 116–121, 123–124, 126, 128–130
train describer 135, 142
train formations 117–119, 124
train heights 145
train indicator 74, 79–81, 98, 111
train radio 140–141
train stop 132, 135, 142
train washing 86, 144
Transport for London 106–107, 147, 156
Travelcard 109
Trilogy of Desire 36
tripcock 132
'tube', word 51
Tube Lines 106–107
tunnel noise reduction 82
tunnel sizes 24, 44, 58
tunnel telephone wires 140–141
tunnelling machines 56, 111
tunnelling rates 21
Twin Rover 109

U-shaped tubes 142
UERL 37–38, 45, 47, 50–51, 70, 74–75, 121
uncoupling 115, 126
uncoupling non–driving motor (UNDM) 126, 129
under-floor equipment 123
UndergrounD 50, 75, 86
Underground Ticketing System (UTS) 108–109
Union Construction Co. 121

ventilation 46, 125
viaducts 11, 59, 63, 65, 83, 93
Victoria 10, 55, 97
Victoria Embankment 14
Victoria Line 42, 97, 101, 106, 108, 125, 129, 146
Vine Street 14, 16–17, 42
Volk's Electric Railway 18

Walworth Road 96
Wapping 104
wartime damage 92
wartime lighting 90
wartime offices 91
wartime sheltering 69, 90–92
wartime wedding 91
Warwick Avenue 61, 145

Waterloo 10, 13, 15–19, 24, 26, 28–29, 30, 33, 42–43, 45, 47, 69, 70, 89, 92–93, 96, 97, 98, 101, 105, 107, 111, 113, 139
Waterloo & City Railway/Line 18, 24, 26, 106, 115, 148
Waterloo & Whitehall Railway 13–18
Watford 55, 57–58, 65, 68, 72, 76, 91, 98, 150
    extension to 57–61
Watford branch (Metropolitan) 68, 72, 78, 148
Watford High Street 55, 65, 72, 99, 134, 136, 144, 146
    Metropolitan station 72
Watford Joint Stock 119–120, 122
Watford Junction 7, 58, 59, 60, 61, 63, 65, 67, 69, 90, 98–99, 104, 108, 114, 118–120, 122, 126, 130, 134–136, 138, 143, 144, 146, 148
Watford Replacement Stock 122–123
Watford route 96, 99, 101, 121, 125, 130, 141
Watford service 67, 119
Watford Stadium 68
Watford West 66
Watkin, Sir Edward William 25, 78
wayleaves 16, 24
weak field 122–124
Wembley, town 76, 79
Wembley Central 63, 122, 135, 139, 156
Wembley Park 58, 78–81, 83–87, 98, 138, 156
West Croydon 112
West End 10–11, 54, 56, 59, 67, 70, 87
West Hampstead 77, 81, 83–84, 145
Westinghouse 132
Westminster 10–11, 13, 23, 72, 82, 106
'White Ladies' 11
Whitehall 10–11, 13–14, 17
Willesden Green 81, 84–85, 138, 156
Willesden Junction 54, 57–60, 62–63, 67, 111, 118, 136, 138, 147, 156
Willesden signal box 134–135, 139
window netting 90
winter 119
Witley Park 27, 33–34
Woolwich Arsenal 104
World War I 59, 66, 69, 112, 120
World War II 69, 88, 94, 104, 112, 120, 125
Wright, James Whitaker 27, 31–34
    bribery of press 32
    lawsuit 33
    prosecution and flight 33
    trial and suicide 33–34
Wright, John 27

Yerkes, Charles Tyson 31, 35–40, 45, 47, 54, 115–117
    blackmail and bribery 35–36
    Chicago 35–36
    death and estate 39, 50
    financial schemes 37–38, 47
    Philadelphia 35
    prosecution and prison 35
    trams 35–36
Yerkes group 39, 41, 44, 46, 52, 115–117, 132, 140
Yerkes (lunar crater) 40
Yerkes Observatory 40
York Road 96
Ypresian 22

Zeppelins 69, 90, 92